AN
EXTRAORDINARY
MIXTURE

by

Stanley G. Bennett

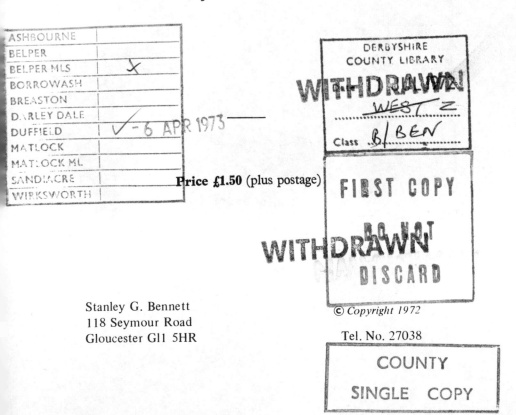

Price £1.50 (plus postage)

Stanley G. Bennett
118 Seymour Road
Gloucester Gl1 5HR

© *Copyright 1972*

Tel. No. 27038

That was a good one!

AN EXTRAORDINARY MIXTURE

"I'm fed up with this place," said one convict to another. "Just because I hit a warder with a shovel the governor won't let me go to choir practice."

Most of the items in this book appeared originally as articles in the Gloucester Journal and Citizen during the past few years, and I wish to thank the Editor for his kind permission to reprint them.

I was born in a Gloucestershire village, but moved with my family to live at Spaxton (Somerset), where my father was appointed organist at the Church. The village was four miles from the nearest town (Bridgwater) and close to the Quantock Hills.

We had a fairly big house, with two orchards adjoining, and a garden of about half an acre. At the bottom of the garden was part of a 15 foot high wall, surrounded the Agapemone, known locally as the Abode of Love. This old mannor house and five acres of land were surrounded by the high wall, and was first occupied by Henry Prince who ruled there for many years before he died in 1899; he lived there with his many women in the prim and prudish Victoria age.

A few years later the Revd. John Hugh Smyth-Pigott stated that he was the Messiah, and he sought sanctuary in the high-walled hide-away of the Agapemone community at Spaxton. He took with him his wife, and a younger woman, Ruth Preece; he explained that Ruth was his "spiritual bride." When Smyth-Pigott became master of the Abode of Love he was unfrocked for "immoral life and habits."

In the early days at Spaxton Ruth bore her "spiritual husband" three children - Glory, Hallelujah, and Power, and I knew the Registrar of Births and Deaths who registered these children.

Henry Prince, who claimed to be the imortal messenger of the Holy Ghost, built the Abode in 1860's - with money provided by his rich female followers.

What a long walk it was to get to school - nearly 2 miles. No food or drink was then available at the school, and if you needed some stimulant it was necessary to take it with you. One of the things I remember when entering the school was seeing the head-master's cane behind the frame of "Love one another."

At the age of ten I first began to take an interest in birds, and for over 70 years the irresistible appeal of Nature has enriched my mind with memories that will never be forgotten. What started this interest was being asked to go with two men to hold a lamp, shinning into a large net one man held up one side of a hedge while the other man went the other side of the hedge and beat it with a large stick, the birds when caught being placed in a large basket. The next

1

day I saw these poor birds flying about in a large wire-netting cage, to be sold for a few pence to those who needed them. Another thing that touched my heart was seeing a bird on the road, alive but unable to fly away. I knocked at the door of a house nearby, and was told that it was a swift, and if I picked it up it would fly. I can still feel the pain I got in my finger from one of its claws but it flew away with 'many thanks'

Ascertaining the positions of nests and their construction; getting to know and appreciate birds songs; the manner of flight, which birds, when danger threatened, were affected by sound and which by movement; noting the wonderful devotion of parent birds to their young and the tremendous efforts to provide them with food - these are a few of the things on which I concentrated.

In those far off days there was not much opportunity to read books on the subject - few were published then - and any knowledge gained was the result of my own observations, but living in the country at that time helped considerably in being able to pursue the most fascinating hobby.

Corncrakes were very plentiful in the year 1900, but although the rasping calls of these very secretive birds were frequently heard they were not often seen, even though one might appear to be standing close to them in the long grass. Each time I hear the dialing tone of the telephone going I am reminded of the bird's call : "Crek, crek."

Finding the first nightingale's nest gave me a tremendous thrill the location of it being my reward for waiting patiently, watching and listening to their songs in a wooded valley for a period covering two breeding seasons. Built of dead leaves and grass in a bank at the bottom of a hedgerow, the nest contained four olive-brown eggs, the wonderful blending of the colours with its surroundings making it difficult to distinguish.

With no pretension of being scientific ornithologists people can get satisfaction in liking birds for their own sake. Even the cheeky sparrow, acrobatic tit, or that great mimic the starling will afford plenty of opportunities for close study, and the singing of the blackbird and thrush gives tremendous pleasure to all who care to listen to them.

One of my acquaintances was a man who used to sit all day by a heap of large stones placed on the grass verge. His job was to break these stones with a hammer into pieces small enough to place on the road when it needed repairing. He wore wire goggles to protect his eyes from flying stones, and if ever a man earned his living by the sweat of his brow this one certainly did! Despite the monotony of the work he was, like most village workers, a very happy and contented man, and he always had an encouraging word for the little boy who passed him daily.

Uneducated and of lowly birth, stone-cracker John possessed great moral qualities and his mode of life set an example to others in the village. Although he knew nothing about music he joined the village band to beat the big drum. During a march his timing was excellent, but due to shortness of stature, a bulging waistline and short arms, he had great difficulty in striking the drum in the centre!

Gone are the days when boys of our village - including myself - used to take off our hats when meeting the Squire, and when one never saw even the ankles of women because they wore boots and long skirts. But I often wonder whether children of to-day, with meals provided and conveyances to take them to school, are any happier than those of my schooldays. We boys got a great deal out of life simply by contributing something towards it by our own efforts. So far as I can remember there was no pocket-money available from the family purse, but there were opportunities to work and earn a few coppers to put in an empty pocket. A farmer would give a boy a small amount for riding the front horse at harvesting time; tying up sheaves of corn; cutting chaff, etc.

A red-letter day for me was receiving half a crown from a farmer for collecting and filling a sack with acorns for the pigs. In those days this was a fortune!! A travelling theatrical company came to Bridgwater for a week; it was known locally as the blood tub. Each night of the week it was there I walked 4 miles, and spent threepence each night for a seat, but on the Saturday afternoon the great Bill Cody was there, and I also went to see this wonderful show. To see six different shows and then to watch Bill shooting bottles in the air was full satisfaction. On the night the Company did the "Face at the Window" I am afraid I looked at every window that I passed on my dark walk home.

A lot of enjoyment was to be had when attending the village sports and watching men climbing up a pole covered in grease. But perhaps two competitions provided for women only caused the greatest amusement. One was supposed to be a donkey race, No saddle or bridle was used, the women sitting astride and facing the hindquarters of the animals, and using an umbrella as a whip. The other was in trying to catch and hold a young pig by the tail, which was well greased!

Most of the villagers went to the annual fair held in Bridgwater, and my earliest recollection of this was buying sixteen walnuts for a penny, and a large ice cream for a halfpenny.

Itinerant performers gave exhibitions in the streets, and we country bumpkins gazed in wonder at the demonstrations they gave for a few coppers. One old negro got a spectator to bind a piece of copper wire around the bicep of his arm, then clenched his fist and flexed his forearm with enough strength to break it; concluding his show by standing with bare feet on red-hot iron. Another man lay on the ground, minus his shirt, then placed a large stone on his chest and invited an onlooker to break it with a sledge-hammer.

Swallowing a watch, while someone held the chain attached, was the speciality of another man; but his piece de resistance was break-ing a lamp glass and swallowing the fragments.

I pulled out a long hat pin - used by most women in those days - from the arm of one performer who pushed it between the muscles.

3

and right through his upper arm.

This, and "all the fun of the fair," provided a boy with all the excitement he could expect in one day, but it did not end there Accepting a ride to my home on a very dark and wet miserable night in a pony-cart we were unfortunate enough to collide with a loaded timber carriage. The shafts of our cart were broken off, four occupants landed in the road, and then the pony ran away. Cut and bruised, we somehow managed to walk the four miles home, but imagine our amazement to find the pony safe in its stable!

Whether the schoolmaster of the village school which I attended was very different from those holding similar positions in other schools I do not know, but "The Gaffer" at mine was an adept in the use of his cane. His method of punishment, besides being very painful to the recipient was very unorthodox, and it would cause much anger among parents of to-day. To make a thorough job of it he called on the assistance of his son, who was a teacher. Desk and seat were joined together in one fixture, and this was used partly as a vice to hold an unwilling victim. A boy due for "ten of the best" stood between the seat and the desk, the son pressing the boy's body down on the desk so that the behind was nicely exposed and tightened for the father's pleasure. The latter, who had a long beard reaching to the lower button of his waistcoat, then applied the cane with such vigour that it must have stopped the ticking of his watch!

Most of the inhabitants of the village used to attend all the services at the local Church. It was here where I used to pump the wind into the organ for my father to play; later I sang in the choir, and then took to do some bell-ringing. And it is the Vicar that I particulary remember as one of those responsible for installing into my young mind the fundamental principles of life.

To get to the Church it was necessary to walk more than two miles along a very lonely road in all kinds of weather, but despite this, the Vicar must have thought my attendances were very good as he gave me a Bible in January 1901 as a special prize for regularity; I still have this good book. So far as I can remember there was only one occasion I failed to attend an evening service, and this was due to very unusual circumstances.

My father and mother set out from home one winter's night to attend the service, telling me to follow them immediately I had locked up the pigs and fed them. One sow was missing, but eventually I found her in a shed grunting as if in considerable pain, It was very dark at the time so I lit a candle and discovered the reason for the noise - a baby pig had arrived! Here was a dilemma for a boy of ten who knew very little about the facts of life - least of all pigs! This was a new experience for me, it seemed that if I remained with the sow it might be some little comfort to her. Each time she gave a big grunt another little pig arrived, and so it continued until my parents returned and found me acting as a sort of midwife. They were delighted to see that their little boy had attached the litter of eight to the "milk bar." As the sow lay stretched out on the straw, it was possible to see, even in the dim light of the candle what appeared to be a look of contentment on her face; or was it one of relief?

4

Another boy and myself were on our way to sing in the choir of the Church, and on the journey we found a Coots nest, from which my pal, after walking along a branch of willow, took two eggs. Piercing the end of one of them he discovered it was addled, and threw it at me.

Unfortunately the smashed egg became embedded in one of my stockings, and although I did my best to clear it away a certain amount remained there, and it was in this condition I took my place in the choir. The smell was dreadful! Several members of the choir raised handkerchiefs to their noses, and I am sure the vicar got 'wind' of it for it seemed that his sermon was shorter than usual; probably he wanted a change of air!

After a period in the choir I was invited to have some lessons in bell-ringing, and what a horrible mess I made of it. Satisfactory progress was made in the preliminary stages, but when attempting to ring a peal one night it proved disastrous, particularly for the five experienced ringers who were taking part. Before a peal can be started, it is first necessary to raise the bells to a position where they will rest with bottoms uppermost; there is a 'stay' at the end of each bell to prevent it turning over. As we pulled the ropes to start the peal the bells swung downwards, and as my bell continued in an upward swing I made an error in failing to check its flight by grasping the rope in the correct position. Not wishing to be taken up to the ceiling with the rope I released it, and the weight of the bell broke the supporting stay and the bell became out of control. To make matters worse the flying rope got entangled with the candelabrum hanging from the centre of the ceiling and snuffed all the candles to put the place in darkness. This was a very awkward situation, but the old experienced ringers clung to their ropes to lower their bells. Suddenly there was a shout from out leader to me to "GET OUT!", and I ran from the place as fast as my legs would carry me.

The day before the relief of Mafeking in South Africa in 1900 I was due for a dose of the headmaster's "medicine" because, when he asked me who I was talking to , I replied that I was talking to myself! "Stand up, he shouted. As he walked to get his cane I noticed that the school door was open, and without any thought of the consequences ran from the school and then hid in a hedge for the remainder of the day. It was the last time I went to school, for I obtained a job in a lawyers office in Bridgwater, and it became necessary to walk four miles each morning and night for the large sum of 3/6 per week. The first day was very eventful. After doing the four miles on foot in pouring rain I arrived at my destination soaked to the skin, but my employer came to my aid by lending me a pair of his long trousers - which needed turning up at the bottom of the legs several times - while my own clothes were dried by the fire in the office.

Most of my employer's clients were farmers and country people. One of my jobs was to make the fire in the morning and keep it going during the day, and in doing this I may have been responsible, without knowing it, for an alarming incident. The

5

coal was stored in a large wooden box in a small back room, and lying on a shelf immediately above the box were several cartridges for a revolver. Incidentally, the two offices had been made from one large room and divided by a thin wooden partition, my "boss" being in one part and I, his Chief Clerk, in the other. On Christmas Eve an elderly farmer came to make a will, and within a few minutes of his occupying a seat near the fireplace there was a terrific explosion!! By some means one of the cartridges had fallen into the coal box, and just before the farmer arrived I had put a shovelful of coal from this box on the fire. Fragments from the fire flew in all directions, and the bullet from the cartridge went through the partition of the room and imbedded itself in a cupboard a few feet from where I was sitting. Fortunately the affair ended without causing any great damage, but it must have been a very uncomfortable experience for both lawyer and client seated so near the unguided missile.

One of the men for whom I always had the greatest respect was my Sunday School teacher; a most cheerful man, with great personality. The boys of his class honoured and admired him for the example he set in his Christian way of life. Twenty years after I left the class I saw him again, when I was on leave from the Army. So great was my admiration for him that when visiting a town (where he was then living) it occurred to me that he may like to see one of his old pupils and I looked forward to meeting him again and having a talk about those early days. But the shock I received when seeing him made me wish that I had never made the journey. Instead of being greeted with that radiant smile I remembered so well from childhood, I saw a very decrepit old man, unshaven and unclean, lying on an old couch. This appeared to be his only furniture, but the number of empty spirit bottles llying round the place left no doubt in my mind as to the cause of my idol's downfall. He did not remember me or my early association with him, and when he resented my intrusion in what can only be described as a hovel I left him, sad with the thought that a man who had once spent so much time in teaching and guiding me along the path of righteousness should have fallen by the wayside.

Here is an instance of a man giving up that terrible habit to become a Christian. Jim Nicholls was an habitual drunkard, the despair of his poor widowed mother with whom he lived. Night after night for some years she had to put up with him arriving home about midnight in a helpless condition. It was the cause of him losing several jobs and, as she relied on him for housekeeping money, it was necessary for her to go short of food on many occasions. This got to a very bad state, so bad that the widow had to apply for poor relief, and a possibility of this kindly old woman going into a workhouse, a very degrading position for one who had done her best to live up to a christian standard of life. When all hope seemed gone fate took a hand in a most unusual way. Jim arrived outside the front door of his home just after midnight, soaked to the skin by torrential rain. As he groped in the dark to open the front door with his latch-key he overturned and fell to the ground. His·condition was such that he could not rise to his feet again, and he remained there all night in pouring rain. The milkman found him there the following morning, and with the help of his mother carried him into the house. Pneumonia caused Jim to spend some weeks in bed, and it must have been during this time that he reflected on the evils of his life for he vowed that he would never touch intoxicating liquor again. And greatly to his credit he kept his vow. It was great comfort to his mother when he joined the Y.M.C.A. and what a joy it was to her when later on he became the Secretary of this noble Association ! I got to know Jim very well a man of noble character. Despite his weakness for many years he had the courage to fight back and gain a worthy place in society.

When I had been at the office for nearly a year a letter was sent to my parents from a local firm of lawyers offering me work in their office at an increased wage. Incidentally, my Boss was articled to this firm before setting up in practice on his own. For some unknown reason he had a grudge against this firm, and when he was shown this letter he went livid with rage. To think they had approached my parents without first consulting him! He replied to their letter, which I typed, as follows:-

Dear Sirs,

Re S. G. Bennett.
Your letter is before me; it will soon be behind me.

Yours truthfully,

T.A.A.

I did the walking from Spaxton to Bridgwater for several months, and then was pleased when my parents decided to move to Bridgwater. It was here Guy Fawkes night was celebrated, perhaps better than any other place in the country. Nearly the whole of the population took an active part in the preceedings and this has been the custom for many years. There were no cinemas, T.V. or radio then; in fact there was not much in the way of entertainment except what might be termed home made. The 5th of November was the most important date on the calendar, and it was celebrated in a manner which could not have been surpassed. As soon as one carnival was over hundreds of people started to save money for the next, and considerable amount was needed to meet the expense.

The local Council participated, and if some of the cost had to be tacked on the rates - I am not sure that they were - there would have been no quibbling about this as everyone had an interest in it. Before Guy Fawkes night all the shops in the main street were boarded up. On the Cornhill, which is near the centre of the town, old boats were taken from the river and heaped up, tar being placed on them to make a good bonfire. At the start of the proceedings a huge procession consisting of every kind of vehicle carrying gangs of Romans, Saxons, Indians, Monks, and representatives of historical periods, in addition to hundreds of people on foot, all in disguise, and visitors who had come to the town by excursion trains. Valuable prizes were given for the best characters in the procession. At the end of this the best feature was to come; the squibbing display given in the main street when one gang competed against another.

This was the most impressive Guy Fawkes night I have ever seen one that lasted from dusk one evening till 5 o'clock the following morning.

It was the custom in Bridgwater - at Christmas time - for the butchers to invite the public to inspect their shops and slaughter-houses to see the beasts that were for sale. A collection box-bearing the words "DON'T FORGET THE ASSISTANTS", was placed in a prominent position for the public to drop a few coopers in. Pigs were displayed; lying on their bellies, with a large orange in theirs mouths.

At the age of 15 I rode an old bicycle from Bridgwater to Ruardean in the Forest of Dean to spend a few days with relatives - a distance of 84 miles. After arriving there my uncle took me to the Speech House Demonstration - a walk of 5 miles. Another 5 miles took me back to his home, and it was a very tired boy who went to bed at night. The journey from Bridgwater entailed many miles of walking up-hill, and going down-hill I could not ride as both brakes were useless. Whatever made me do this long journey I do not know; probably the spirit of adventure, and an urge to accomplish something difficult.

My father (born in the Forest of Dean) decided that he wanted to return to his native country; we went to live in Cinderford. While living there I secured a job with the Forest of Dean Stone Firms at Parkend, and had to travel there each day on the train. It was here that we bought the cheapest coal I have ever heard of, paying 3/- a ton when sending one of our lorries to the pit to collect it. This was also used for the fire in my office. The first class men were paid eightpence an hour for working on the stone, and with a 53 hour week this amounted to the sum of £1.15.4. Each Friday I went to the Bank at Coleford and drew out about £600, and often I was the only one travelling on the train. The firm I worked for had bought some quarries at Dartmoor, and I was sent there to look after their interest. (Page 1. A boy's working life begins on Dartmoor). Fortunately I did not stay there long, my employers finding it more convenient to send me to the main office in Plymouth, where it proved a wonderful place for me to live, never having been in a big town before.

Here I met an old Scotsman, who was the draughtsman, and what a fine chap he was ! He was mathematician; poet; musician; with a wonderful knowledge of the Bible. He would challenge anyone on biblical subjects; corresponded with Sir Robert Ball on astronomy, and Oxford University regarding the Gaelic language. He took me to the Museum to see the 'wicked' Bible, enclosed in a glass case. Underlined in red ink was the 7th Commandment, the word 'not' being omitted from 'Thou shalt not commit adultery " The firm for which I worked owned quarries at Dartmoor, and De Lank in

Cornwall, and it was my job to take the wages to these places each week.

The best thing I ever did in Plymouth was to join the Y.M.C.A., for this brought me in touch with some of the finest men I ever met, especially in their 'gym' where I was able to carry on with my fitness. They had a house at Whitsands, and we spent many happy week-ends there, buying our provisions at nearby Cawsand Bay. After leaving Plymouth I returned to Whitsand Bay in 1914 for a week's most enjoyable holiday with several of my old chums, and there I experienced something which could not have been foreseen. I had walked about a mile from the camp clad in shirt, slacks, and shoes, when I was questioned by a man it proved to be a detective: as to my identity. My tousled' appearance not satisfying him he accompanied me back to the camp for further investigation. The other members of the party were able to satisfy the detective as to my identification and movements. He then told us that a murder had been committed in the district and search was being made for a man without a hat. I seemed to fit this description all right, but it was a great relief when he accepted our statements and left the camp. Certainly my apprearance justified him in thinking I looked capable of committing a crime, for on that rugged coast line we never cared much about dress or the lack of it !

As the firm I worked for had gone into liquidation for half a million pounds I was dismissed by the receiver. From Plymouth I then moved to Bristol and had a transfer from the local Y.M.C.A. to the Bristol branch, and it was due to the fact that I joined the local cricket side that I was able to get a job in the Post Office Telephones.

During the time I resided there I used to go to the Broad-mead Chapel for the special sermons that the Revd. Benskin used to preach once a fortnight. These sermons were very special, and if you did not get there well before the opening time you failed to get in ! It was the only place that I have visited that I heard clapping in a place of worship.

I was able to join the Bristol Rugby team, and in the first match against the Gloucester team missed kicking four penalty goals !

After being at the office for some time I had to leave - because I was not established - and my place was taken by a man working in the Department in London who had fallen in love with one of the Bristol operators. Something must have gone wrong with this love affair, for after being in Bristol for a few nights he decided to put his head in a gas oven !!

Then I heard of a job going in Gloucester for a Wayleave Officer, and having applied for it was accepted, where I remained for over 40 years, apart from four years service in the 1914-1918 war. For some years after I retired in 1954 - at the age of 65 - I went to live in London for a few years, but I be-

9

came rather tired of the surroundings, and the lack of knowing anyone but my wife, so we then decided to come back to live in the City again.

Benjiman Partridge in "Tom Jones"

A BOYS WORKING LIFE BEGINS ON DARTMOOR

What would the modern boy say if he was offered a job on Dartmoor, and had to leave a comfortable home for the first time and go to that very bleak place in the middle of the winter ?

Yet, at the age of 18, this was my venture into what can be truly described as "outer space".

On arrival at a village near Tavistock I secured lodgings with a Mrs. Bray, a relative of the famous evangelist Billy Bray, the one who once said that if God intended man to smoke he would have put a chimney up through his head.

Never shall I forget the first morning when I had to walk four miles across the moor to get to the office of some quarries.

The weather could not have been worse as I plodded up a long hill to reach a point about 1,600ft. above sea level.

Not a hedge, tree, or human being was to be seen en route; Dartmoor ponies and huge granite boulders were the only things visible through the heavy mist.

Soaked to the skin with rain, I must have looked a terrible sight when presenting myself to the manager in a little office constructed of sheets of corrugated iron. It did seem that this was the last place on earth for there was no sign of habitation anywhere.

This was, indeed a day to remember, for during blasting operations a piece of granite flew into the air and then crashed through the roof of the "tin hut" to fall within a few feet of the fire where I had stripped and was drying my wet clothes !

The manager (called "Mac") was a big raw-boned Scot from the Highlands, cock-eyed and left-handed, who was married to a tiny woman from the Lowlands of Scotland; her fingers were so small that a wedding ring had to be specially made to fit her.

They had 11 children and "Mac" was the most patient and gentle father imaginable, but he was a very different man in his dealings with the workmen.

On one occasion a man who was working on a crane threatened to punch his nose, so he was invited to step down and do it. Before he had time to carry out his threat "Mac" seized him by the scruff of the neck and the seat of his pants and pushed him head first into a barrel of water.

For a considerable time there had been a feud between "Mac" and an Irish workman, and one day I was startled to see "Mac" lying on the ground with "Pat" sitting astride his chest, holding aloft in his right hand a heavy steel tram-shoe and threatening to put an end to "Mac"

But fortunately several workmen saw the danger and prevented what might have been a tragedy.

There were a few incidents in my first boarding-house which will always be remembered. Another boarder shared a bedroom with me; a very nice chap who did some rather unusual things.

I have never seen anyone with so many warts on the hands, and the way he got rid of them must have been a very painful one.

Each night in the bedroom, he would push the point of a needle in the centre of each one and then place the other part of the needle in the flame of a candle. For two minutes the red-hot needle was allowed to burn the wart. The smell reminded me of a blacksmith's shop when a hot shoe is being fitted to a horse's hoof.

Another smell to pollute the air came form the camphorated oil which he used to massage his injured knee each night, and I was jolly thankful when he hopped into bed and read a few passges from the Bible.

He was a good-living Christian, but he did something one night that must have troubled him for a long time.

In the winter the landlady was in the habit of leaving the oven door (attached to the fireplace) open and her black cat used this very warm place to sleep in. Joe came in late one night, not knowing the cat was in the oven, and closed the door.

The grief of the landlady can be imagined when she opened the oven door the next morning and discovered the cat had been suffocated.

This tragedy happened two days after she had read in a newspaper that a ship on which her husband had been a member of the crew for many years—had foundered and all hands lost!

During the six months I lived at this house the landlady wore mourning clothes, but on the day I was leaving the "missing" husband arrived home!

Needless to say it was a terrible shock to the "widow"

When the husband left home to go to sea, his wife naturally thought that he was going to join his usual ship, but for some unknown reason he "signed on" for another one and travelled around the coast of Australia without ever communicating with her.

*   *   *

A UNIQUE CRICKET STORY—THAT'S THE

ONLY THING TO CALL IT

When the secretary of our team wrote to one in another district asking for a fixture with his team, he replied that it would be a pleasure to give us a game, naming the date, and adding: " "You will find our cricket-pitch unique".

12

As we had never played a game of cricket on a pitch so described every member of our team was anxious to see it. In fact, it was almost the sole topic of conversation on the day we travelled to play the match.

After our arrival we changed into white flannels in an old skittle alley attached to the "Live And Let Live,' and then had to walk and carry our gear to the field which was a mile away.

And when we set eyes on this pitch we all agreed that it was unique!

A considerable amount of rain had fallen during the past week and turned the ground into a quagmire. A dozen heavy carthorses and several cows were still in the field, and it seemed that these animals had spent most of their time on the pitch having a rock-and-roll session !

Before the wicket could be marked out and the stumps put in it was necessary to drive the animals away, but they were very reluctant to move.

It was proposed to roll the pitch but the heavy roller was so embedded in the swamp that united efforts of our opponents failed to shift it from its position.

Having won the toss our captain decided to bat and hope for the best.

On one side of the pitch the ground sloped up at such an acute angle that it was possible for a ball to be hit up the hill and then roll down to the pitch again assuming, of course, that it did not stick in the mud!

About 30 yards on the other side was a large pond, and behind the bowler's arm were large elm trees which made it difficult to see a ball when delivered in the very bad light existing.

In addition, the animals kept returning to the region of the pitch, and the men fielding were kept busy trying to drive them away.

At the end of the first over, during which the ball either slithered along the ground or flew over the batsmen's heads, a tremendous thunder-storm descended on us and with no place for shelter, we were soon soaked to the skin.

It was in this state that we trudged wearily back to the changing quarters, and then tried to have a "rub down" with our handkerchiefs.

With some discomfort we all sat down on beer barrels and empty cases to have some refreshment, tea, and huge chunks of bread on which we spread jam with a wooden spoon from a large jar containing enough for both teams.

*   *   *

The Vagabond King (Cheltenham)

OUR VILLAGE CRICKET HAD PLENTY OF LIFE

I took part in village games, the batsmen and bowlers may not have been considered first-class, but they played cricket, and even if the pitches on which we played were rough at times these were the things we expected, and adapted ourselves to the conditions.

There was a great team spirit and generally good sportsmanship; on two occasions only do I remember incidents which did not come under the latter category.

One was when our team was playing away with only ten men, but the captain was able to pursuade a local man to complete the eleven. The time arranged to draw stumps was at 7 o'clock.

Just before this time all our own members had been dismissed, and we needed one run to win when the local man went out to bat

As he walked across the field the church clock struck 7.0, and the wicket-keeper (who was captain of our opponents) pulled the stumps out of the ground and hurried away with them to the pavilion.

The other was when Lord — captained our opponents; he created a very unfavourable impression.

Batting first for his team he had his middle stump knocked out of the ground by the first ball he received.

So disgusted was he that for the rest of the game he sat in his car and read a book, leaving his other ten men to field during our innings.

He must have thought it was his unlucky day when one of our players hit a beautiful 'cow-shot' over square-leg and smashed one of the headlamps of his car!

One of the games provided an unexpected ending after a day's outing to Weston-super-Mare to play a local side. Batting first our score amounted to 89.

At the end of the innings a member of the opposing side said to the captain: "what are you going to do, skipper?" He replied: "I think we'll have a knock and then put them in again."

Satisfied with the reply, this member, and another, left the ground and went by car into the town, quite confident that the team, without them, could easily get a couple of hundred runs and there was no need for them to return hurriedly.

But what a shock they received when they did return—after the game was completed! We dismissed the remaining members for 46, and although the groundsman and his assistant were allowed to complete the team the two 'ducks' they collected made no difference to the total score.

During the course of a game a player from Stow-on-the-Wold hit a ball in my direction, fielding at point, and started to run to the other end.

Suddenly he realised that I had the ball and then turned back and made a head-long dive towards the wickets.

As he did so I threw the ball at them and, very unfortunatly for him the ball hit him a terrible blow at the back of the ear.

He was carried to the pavillion and lay unconscious there for two hours, and it was a great relief to our team, and me in particular, when he recovered.

At the age of 18 someone considered my bowling good enough to warrant a trial in a County Colts match, but after taking part in the game my head was bowed in shame.

Full of confidence I delivered the first ball, only to see it go out of the ground and smash the slates on a house. The next ball went in the same direction, this time going extensive damage to a greenhouse.

Where the next ball went no one knows for it sailed over the boundary fence and was never found!

Undaunted by such treatment I had a ball "up my sleeve" which was going to smash this impudent batsman's stumps into sawdust, but all hope of bowling it was lost when torrential rain put an end to the day's play.

*   *   *

VILLAGE CRICKET THE BEST

I regard the days when taking part in games around the countryside villages as the best of all.

Each member did his share towards cutting the grass, rolling the pitch and marking it, and if it meant a journey on foot or cycle for two or three miles to do it this was all part of our enjoyment, and by our own efforts we achieved something which gave us great satisfaction.

There were no 'buses for transport to away matches and many miles had to be done on bicycle, but occasionally it was possisible to go by horse-driven conveyances.

Due to a mistake by our secretary regarding fixtures with two teams—in one season—journeys of 10 and 16 miles were made without playing the matches.

On arriving at the first of these places we found the field full of sheep and the local team just departing to play another team in the Forest of Dean.

At the end of the other journey we arrived at the ground to see our opponents already playing another team.

I have no record of the lowest score ever made in local cricket, but to my knowledge one village team was dismissed for a total of one—and that was a leg-bye!

Some of the village umpires made queer decisions at times and often had a tendency to favour their own teams, but their interpretation of the rules was amusing; particularly one at Apperley.

One of the bowlers was no-balled with the last ball of the over, and then proceeded to deliver another ball. Before he finished his run up to the wicket the square-leg umpire ran from his position and shouted to the other umpire; "Ere! 'e's 'ad 'is six balls;"

In another game Fred Harris, our best bowler, was standing next to me in the slips and became very disgruntled when the captain put on another player to bowl "donkey-drops."

After the first two balls had been hit for six I heard Fred use words of a profane nature because he had not been put on to bowl, but when the next ball was hooked into an adjoining river for another six Fred could not withhold his thoughts any longer and shouted to the captain: "What's the good of bowling that blooming stuff;'tis like feeding carrots to a donkey!"

Another humorous remark was made during a game in the Forest of Dean when a player used the "long-handle" to hit three sixes and a couple of fours.

Before the bowler delivered the last ball his captain said to him: "Jarge, thou's got'n guessin' any way; now 'im don't know whether to 'it thee for a six or a four!"

Such was a village cricket game in my day, and if at times unusual decisions were made by local umpires, and strange comments sometimes made by the players, the matches were played in the true spirit of the game, and long may it continue.

* * *

A BEAUTIFUL BIRD BUT IT LIVES IN A HOVEL

During the summers when I lived in a bungalow on the side of Gloucester-Sharpness Canal the birds that give me a great deal of pleasure were the kingfishers.

Getting up early on bright sunny mornings was the best time to see them. As they perched on branches that hung low over the water I thought that no other bird in this country could surpass their wonderful plumage of blues, greens, and red, sparkling and reflecting the brightness of the sunshine.

As a member of the rowing club I was able to have access to a boat, and it was this that enabled me to find, over a period of years, several nest-holes in the high banks opposite the towpath, particulary between the Two-Mile Bend and the Pilot Inn.

17

The holes, or tunnels, are made rather small at the entrance and then broaden inside, with a chamber at the end for a "nest".

From the entrance to the chamber there is a slight upward trend and, presumably, the wise birds take this precaution to ensure that the drainage is in the right direction.

In all the holes I found there was never an indication that any kind of "nest" was made before the eggs were laid , but when the eggs were hatched there was a mat of fishbone pellets underneath the young birds.

This could have been made when the parents were feeding the brood, throwing up the bones so that they fell between the young to be trodden on and form a "nest."

The accummulation of these fish-bones in a confined space created a very unpleasant smell, and when the parent birds, after feeding, emerged quickly from this foul place and dived straight in to the water it may have been to cleanse themselves!

There were only two bungalows on the canal banks during my residence, and in the very peaceful surroundings a pair of king-fishers chose a near-by bank to make a nesting-hole.

Having to get to business each day somewhat restricted my time but in the early mornings I was able to watch these birds— from a window—as they in turn attacked the bank with their very strong beaks and excavated the soil to make the tunnel.

Eventually the work was completed, and some weeks later I had the pleasure of seeing the parent birds taking food to their young in the nest-holes and on the overhanging branches.

But what impressed me greatly was the manner in which the food was obtained.

The parents perched on low branches near the water where they could watch minnows and other small fish swarming around the roots of the bushes.

Suddenly they would plunge headlong into the water, secure the fish and return to the perch to kill it. Then they would flash like a meteor above the water to disappear into the nest-hole with-out, apparently decreasing their speed.

It is not surprising that such a beautiful bird has been the theme for myth and folk-lore. For centuries it was believed that the king-fisher—its olden name was Halcyon—made a nest which floated on the open sea.

Another legend was that the bird, if kept damp, would not decay and if hung by the beak would renew its feathers year by year.

If the skin or body of a dead kingfisher was hung by a single thread the beak always pointed to the quarter whence the wind was blowing, was another old belief, and it was not unusual to find one of these birds hanging from a ceiling in a country cottage.

"But how now stands the wind ?

18

Into what quarter peer
my Halcyon's bill ?"

*   *   *

THE PEOPLE I'VE MET IN THE COUNTRY

For many years I travelled the Gloucestershire district interviewing
people of the countryside regarding the erection of H.M. telegraphs
on private property, and during that time had experience of unusual
incidents and heard may stories ranging form pathos to humour, the
latter not always being intentional.

Of the unusual incidents some come readily to mind.

After ringing the bell at a large mansion in Andoversford a lady—
the owner—opened the door, and on seeing me she called to the
maid upstairs: "Mary, here's the man from the steam laundry."

A maid at Wotton-under-Edge opened the door slightly without
revealing herself and said : "We shan't want any coal today, thank
you."

First a laundryman, and now a coalman, thought I, but worse was
to follow

At Ashchurch a woman didn't even trouble to answer the door
when I knocked, but shouted from her kitchen: "I don't want no
pegs." Lifting the lid of her letter-box I explained my business and
when she realised I wasn't a 'gypo' she was most profuse in her
apoligies.

Perhaps one of my most awkward experiences was in trying
to persuade three elderly maiden sisters to grant permission for
lopping a tree; the latter was overhanging a road and prevented the
erection of a telephone route. The maidens were all very deaf.
One held an ear-trumpet while I explained my business in stentorian
tones, and then I had to repeat this procedure with the others in
turn via the trumpet.

They then conferred with each other, aided by the trumpet,
but all my efforts were of no avail. they would not give consent.

A man who occupied an old railway carriage erected on a grass
verge asked me if is was possible to move a stay near his residence.
As it was on the highway I told him it could not be done, "Well,"
he said, "if you can't move it I'll ask the Lord; the Lord's good,
and he'll get it moved". Perhaps his prayer was unheard; the stay
was still there 30 years later.

Mrs. Smith, normally residing in London, rented a cottage
which she used for occasional visits. She complained of wires crossing
her garden, and when I called on her regarding this she said: I expected the Postmaster General to call on me," and slammed the
door in my face.

That she was very unpopular in the village can be judged from the following incident told me by the local Postmaster.

The vicar, a very kindly and genial man, walked through the snow on Christmas Eve and put a seasonal greetings cards into her letter-box. A day or so later he received a very abusive letter from this ungrateful person threatening to prosecute him if he again trespassed on her property!

Writing of clergy brings to mind some of the quaint—and true—sayings of country lay preachers in chapels arround the Gloucester district.

Although some countrymen use words quite other than those thought to be correct they still manage to convey their meaning.

A local preacher prefaced his sermon by saying: "I can't exactly put my hand on my text for to-night off-hand, but 'tis somewhere within this good old book — 'England expects, etc." while another gave out his text: "Lowce'n and let'n goa". (Loose him and let him go)

At the close of this service he said to a fellow preacher' "Ah, Mr. Williams, what a lot of champaigns you and I have had to-gether".

In a chapel I attended on several occasions the pulpit protruded over two front rows of seats.

When a local man, Tom Evans, took the service, generally twice a year, people avoided these seats it possible because when using words like Pontius Pilate he laid such stress on the P's that spittle from his mouth flew in all directions.

When he was asked to take the harvest festival service most of the vegetables surrounding the pulpit were the produce from Tom's garden. "My sermon tonight" said Tom, "will be about the good seed of this 'ere land."

During the sermon he seemed to ignore all the stops and commas, pausing only when it was necessary to take breath, ending with these words: "If any of you d'want any seed potatoes I can let you 'ave some for a bob a peck."

*   *   *

OPERATIC MEMORIES (LARGELY COMIC)

OF GLOUCESTER'S AMATEUR STAGE

Gloucester should be proud to have such an extremely good amateur theatrical organisation as the local Operatic and Dramatic Society, the members of which, by their enthusiasm and hard work, provide the public with first-class entertainment each year.

During my residence in the city one of the greatest pleasures

I had was being a member of the Gloucester Operatic and Dramatic Society for 35 years. Although no longer an active member I am a life member who still takes the greatest interest in the functions of the Society which provided me with so much enjoyment, and created innumerable friendships.

Why I joined in 1918 is not quite clear, for I had no previous stage experience, and my voice—if any—had been ruined by continually shouting orders during the 1914-1918 war.

" Dorothy" was the light opera chosen for the year, and Messrs. Chance and Llewellyn Bland (of "The Citizen") and W. P. Cullis were the men who selected the principals. The proper course for me should have been to serve an apprenticeship in the chorus, but I had the audacity to try for the principal comedy part of 'Lurcher' and, greatly to the consternation of old members and myself got it!

A feature of the show was the appearance on the stage of the Master of the Arle Court Beagles and some of his hounds at each performance, and with members suitably attired in hunting costumes it provided a wonderful spectacle.

I had to speak some lines about Windsor soap, and at the Friday evening performance officers from the RAOC—then at the Docks—sat in a box at the Hippodrome, and when reference was made to the soap they threw down several tablets at me on the stage!

There was a 'hold-up' at one performance because, when trying to make a quick change behind the scene I was unable to get into my breeches; one of the women had sewn up the legs!

In "Ruddigore" large pictures (in heavy frames) of ancestors formed the back-ground of some scenery, and during one scene male members — attired like the ancestors—stood behind the frames, When the stage lights were extinguished the frames were pulled up and disappeared, and as the lights came on again the audience saw live 'ancestors' standing like statues.

During the Saturday matinee one of the pictures stuck half-way up, with the man still behind it and only legs exposed to view. I was on stage speaking to the ancestors, and just as I came to the words 'my fathers, wallowers in blood' the man behind the half-exposed picture ducked underneath it and stood up, absolutely killing the illusion. This was real comic opera!!

NO PRODUCER OF GILBERT AND SULLIVAN OPERAS WILL ALLOW ANY ALTERATION TO THE ORIGINAL DIAL—OGUE, BUT I HAVE KNOWN A FEW EXTRA WORDS AND EFFECTS GET IN BY ACCIDENT.

In the first presentation of "The Yeomen of the Guards" at Gloucester a well-known resident played the part of the headsman and he was well-suited physically for it. On the first night he had to come on stage carrying his axe, and then, as the bell tolled, proceed to the chopping block between two rows of warders and bring the axe down with a thud on the block. With all

Wilfred Shadbolt in the Yeomen of the Guard

his strength he delivered the blow, but missed the block, and what we and all the audience heard was a loud cry of: Oh! my bloody foot!!"

There is an unaccompained quartet in "The Yeomen" entitled 'Strange Adventure!' The orchestra plays a few bars before the commencement to enable the quartet's soprano, Kate, to pitch the correct note, and in the production at the Hempsted Village Hall poor Kate must have experienced a very 'strange adventure.' A barge was proceeding along the canal during the performance, and to give warning for the canal bridge to be opened a terrific blast was given on a siren, the sound arriving at the hall just at the moment the orchestra completed the opening bars. The sound was so great that the quartet never heard the last note of music and took their cue from the siren!

When playing the part of 'Wilfred Shadbolt' in "The Yeomen" I, encountered one 'Jack Point' who played havoc with the dialogue. We were singing the well known 'Cock and Bull' duet, and this goes at such a speed there is not much time to take breath. I was singing the words 'Down I dived into the river,' but before I could complete' 'But alas I cannot swim' from the side of Jack Point's mouth came these outrageous words: 'You silly ass, you can't swim a stroke.' W. S. Gilbert who wrote the words of the opera would have turned in his grave!

One man in the chorus thought he should play a principal part, so he was given one in 'Princess Ida.' His first appearance was in a trio, of which I was one.

We wore very heavy armour and as we walked down the stage the armour of the new principal rattled as he trembled inside. He was supposed to sing the first two lines, but they never came and I had to sing them for him to save an awkward situation. Never again did he try to take a principal part!

There is one painful memory I have of "Tom Jones" when playing the part of "Benjamin Partridge." Trying to fall down the stairs too realistically on the opening night I did not anticipate a large nail which protruded from the side and a deep gash the length of my leg caused a good deal of trouble for the rest of. the week.

Two weeks before our performance of "The Rebel Maid" the late Ben Price, the producer and myself, went to Bristol in the producer's old car to see the local Society's production of this show. This old car was not capable of doing more than 20 miles an hour, and it was just as well when we met a very formidable obstacle on the return journey.

Had the road been clear on this moonlight night all would have been well, but near Berkeley Road an avenue of trees threw shadows across it to blot out the vision. And then it came—crash !

A big cart horse was moving across the road, and the car hit it broadside and carried it on the bonnet for some yards before it struggled off and disappeared. Before the producer got out of the car to assess the damage his first words were: "Blast it ! I havent got the damned thing insured."

One of the best and most conscientious members we ever had was the late Reg Dutton, and when he played a part his aim was to get perfection. At the St. Aldate Hall he was taking part in a play and using all his skill to bring out the dramatic situations, but a little incident happened off stage that ruined his performance and caused him great distress.

During his speech that was delivered almost in a whisper, with an enthralled audience and a very tense atmosphere, some fool chose that particular moment to pull the chain' not five yards away, and the 'noises off' of water being flushed filled the auditorium!

An amusing thing happened when a London woman joined the Society. It was the usual practice to distribute tickets to members for sale to their friends and other people, and this new member was given tickets to the value of £5. Two days later she asked the secretary to give her some more. He said "You have done exceptionally well to sell so many tickets in such a short time." "Sell them," she said, "I haven't sold them. I thought they were to be given away!"

My last appearance was very disastrous. Playing the part of 'Don Alhambra' in "The Gondoliers" I had to walk on stage and announce to the whole company that the Prince's foster-mother had been found.

It was the concluding performance on Saturday night and wishing to give great emphasis to the words., I yelled at the top of my voice, not "the Prince's foster-mother has been found but "the praunces fister-mother has been found!!" What a climax to a long career!

*   *   *

DOUBLE BARREL. A child was being christened, and the District Nurse was standing next to the Vicar at the Font. She said: "The child's name sir, is Smith Peterson. Said the Vicar: "Is it hyphenated?" The Nurse replied: "Yes sir, the doctor did it on Tuesday".

ANNOUNCEMENT A famous singer was staying in Somerset, and had promised to sing at the village concert,.The local blacksmith, hearing this, called on the singer and asked him if he was going to sing the "Village Blacksmith", because, if so, would he mention that he repaired bicycles as well."

"Lurcher" in Dorothy   *First appearance in 1919*

I SAW A WOODPECKER DRUMMING

During the second week in April a friend and myself visited a wood where I found the nests of woodpeckers in previous years.

It is at this time of the year that these birds become very active in making new holes or enlarging old ones for nesting.

Many trees were found containing holes, but it was not until we arrived at the edge of the wood that we noticed a great spotted woodpecker at work on the hole in a large treee.

As it was possible that this could be for a nest-hole it was decided to stay in the vicinity and keep the bird and hole under observation.

Very convenient for doing so was a bush overhanging a dry ditch, and after reinforcing this with a quantity of leafy elder we had a suitable "hide."

Generally woodpeckers choose trees that are hollow or partly so, but this particular tree appeared to be a sound one; buds all over it were bursting into leaf.

After sitting in the "hide" for a considerable time we saw the woodpecker return to the hole and continue to excavate chips of wood from the tree, drumming the whole time it did so.

This drumming has always been a puzzle to me, for I could never understand if it was caused by the bird's beak hitting the tree or some kind of guttural sound emanating from the bird.

To try to satisfy my curiosity I decided on a little experiment.

While the bird continued to drum my companion quietly left the "hide" and walked to a position at the other end of the wood, a distance of approximately 250 yards.

The conditions were ideal for sound to be heard—apart from the singing of the birds, there was no other noise to distract the attention; the wind, too, was blowing in the right direction.

The bird was still hammering on the tree when my friend returned, and he assured me that he had heard the drumming very distinctly.

I asked him to go to the same place again and listen while I tapped on the tree.The hole in the tree was about 20 feet from the ground and not difficult to reach by making use of the many branches available for climbing.

When my companion reached his destination he shouted for me to start the experiment.

The only thing I had that slightly resembled the beak of a woodpecker was a small pocket-knife, and the handle of this was used to strike some staccato blows as hard as possible on the tree near the hole for two minutes. But this sound was not heard by my collaborator.

Incidentally, the sound of a woodpecker drumming has been heard at a distance of threequarters of a mile.

The bird we were watching is only slightly larger than a starling, and we came to the conclusion that a bird of this size could not make as much noise with its beak alone as I did with the handle of the knife.

Since then I have been able to see, on three occasions, the wonderful film of woodpeckers made by Heinz Sielmann, and have no reason for altering my opinion regarding the drumming.

We were also fortunate enough to see from our "hide" that interesting little bird the nuthatch, busy filling up the entrance to a big hole in another tree.

This is done with mud or clay until the entrance is just big enough for the use of this small bird. What hard work it must entail!

One nest—taken from a haystack—was given to the British Museum, and in the construction of this 1 1lb. of clay was used!

*   *   *

GET RID OF THE WING FORWARDS!

After watching the 'Varsity match between Oxford and Cambridge I began to wonder if spectators are ever going to have the opportunity of seeing the real game as it should be played.

For although it was originally intended as a handling game, it now seems that it has developed into one of kicking on every possible occasion, and an important point is that when indiscriminate kicking is done the team doing so loses possession of the ball.

I feel confident that wing-forwards are detrimental to the game; there is nothing constructive in their play, Their object seems to be to stop the fly half at all costs, and as their value in the scrum is negligible they are just hangers-on-real parasites!

Even if they do do not stop the fly-half they force him across the field in such a manner that all the threequarters bunch together with no chance of making headway.

I FEEL REALLY SORRY FOR THE WING THREEQUARTERS WHAT OPPORTUNITIES DO THEY GET, AND HOW OFTEN DO THEY SCORE TRIES, IN THE GAME AS PLAYED TODAY?

A few years ago when fly-half Sharp cut through the centre on a few occasions in an international match at Twickenham it created a sensation! Perhaps to the younger generation but to the older people it was not so, for they remembered games of many years ago when brilliant back play was a feature of the games and to beat an opponent like Sharp did was a very ordinary occurrence.

"Tabarie" in the Vagabond King

I am sure there are a great many good threequarters to-day, but when impeded by roaming wing-forwards and forced towards the touch-line they will never get an opportunity to develop their play.

THE REMEDY ? REDUCE THE NUMBER OF PLAYERS TO THIRTEEN AND DISPENSE WITH WING-FORWARDS, MAKING MORE SPACE AVAILABLE ON THE FIELD AND A CHANCE FOR MORE OPEN PLAY.

When I saw the last County match at Kingholm between Gloucestershire and Devon it was one continuous forward maul.

At the time I felt that if I had gone into the cattle market that day and collected sixteen bullocks they could have done as well as those forwards!

I do not possess a copy of the rules, but my scheme regarding the scrummage would make it easy for the referee, and plain enough for the spectators to understand.

With six forwards only, packing three, two, one, make a rule that ONLY the centre man of each front row be allowed to raise his foot to hook the ball; any other player would be penalised.

Also make it an offence if either scrum-half encroaches on his opponents side of the scrum.

With his type of pack the ball should be heeled quickly form the scrum to the scrum-half, and play opened up immediately.

With no interference from wing forwards, and more space in which the backs can move, we should get fast runners, in possession of the ball, with opportunities for dummies, side-stepping, or swerving, in fact doing everything legitimate to out-wit their opponents, just like the Gloucester backs used to do 50 years ago.

Who remembers the thrills we had in watching wing-threequarter Arthur Hudson score so many brilliant tries ? I think he would be the first to admit that much of his success was due to the clever play of half-backs and centre threequaters who first evaded their opponents before giving him a pass to race for the line. Is it too much to hope that we shall ever see the like again ?

There are far too many scrummages in the game to-day. To eliminate some of these I would suggest that when a man is tackled in possession of the ball and it is not playable, allow the player to stand up (with his back to the opposition) and pass the ball to any one of his team-mates.

Many infringements happen in the line-out, for which a scrum is ordered, and here again more open play would result if the team entitled to the ball were allowed to start a handling movement, but it should be an offence if the player who receives the first pass kicked it into touch again.

These are a few suggestions that might help to brighten up the game and give more entertainment to the spectators.

Had I the opportunity I would experiment with only 26 players on the field, and try out the simple rules which have been suggested, for if anything is needed to bring back the game to its former glory it is to get rid of the present kick-and-rush tactics—and particularly those objectionable wing-forwards!

For those who like figures here are some I wrote down when watching the Oxford and Cambridge match. In the first half the ball was kicked into touch on 50 occasions, and 36 in the second half (a total of 86), many of them needlessly. Infringements from the lines-out were responsible for 24 scrums and nine penalty kicks.

*   *   *

BESS THE RETRIEVER CAME BACK WITH THE TROUSERS

Bess the labrador did not possess any qualities that would enable her to win prizes for her good looks at a dog show, nor did she have a pedigree, but she was bred from parents that had made history by their retrieving, and Bess had inherited these to a very high degree.

Among shooting men in the Gloucestershire countryside she was recognised as the best gundog in the area, and after a day with her in the field she would be the sole topic of conversation among those privileged to see her at work.

When other dogs were sent out to retrieve a wounded rabbit or a running pheasant they often failed to find them, but it was a very rare event if Bess did not find fur and feather and bring them to hand.

Perhaps the best retrieving she ever did was described to me by her owner, Bill Cox, when he and a friend set out (60 years ago) with a pony cart to drive from Gloucester to Marlborough, the dog accompanying them.

Bill intended to break the journey at Cirencester and stay the night with a friend, who was the landlord of a public-house.

At the top of Birdlip Hill Bill alighted and took a half-crown form his pocket and dipped it into some aniseed. He then took Bess to a spot near a wall and gave her a sniff of the coin, and, so that she could see what he was doing then covered the coin with a stone. The idea was to send the dog for it when the party arrived at Cirencester.

Bill told me that he had done similar things on several occasions and won a few bets on the results.

While the two friends were having some light refreshment in the public-house a traveller named George—well known to Bill—dropped in before driving on towards Gloucester.

During a conversation Bill told him about the coin he had hidden at Birdlip for the dog to retrieve, but George laughed at this, and offered to bet a £1 that it could not be done. The bet was accepted and the dog sent out on its mission.

Soon afterwards the traveller set out on his journey, and driving a very fast pony he was able to overtake the dog en route.

On his arrival at Birdlip he pulled up and awaited the dog, his mind set on a scheme to outwit the animal with his own, as he thought superior ingenuity.

It was getting dark as the dog arrived, but just light enough to watch her searching for the stone, and as she moved from one to another George followed close behind.

When the correct stone was located the dog made an effort to turn it over, but before she succeeded in doing so George snatched it away, picked up the coin and put it in a pocket of his trousers and drove off to continue his journey.

As he descended the hill he thought how clever he had been, unaware that Bess had done a bit of quick thinking and was closely following him underneath the pony-cart.

The traveller intended staying the night at a public-house in Hucclecote, and it was quite dark when he arrived in the yard to hand over the pony to the ostler, without catching sight of Bess.

The ostler did see her, and thinking she belonged to George he gave her food and drink and found sleeping quarters for her in the stable.

But Bess could not rest, so when the traveller retired to his bed for the night she ascended the stairs in a search for him. There were only two bedrooms available for travellers, and it was a bit of good fortune for the dog that the door of George's bedroom was partly open.

His trousers had been placed on the back of a chair—something the dog could not see in the darkness—and Bess had no difficulty in finding them once the strong smell of aniseed reached her nostrils.

She pulled the trousers down, and although she was unable to extract the coin from them she did the next best thing—took trousers and coin and delivered them to her owner in Cirencester early next morning.

I never heard who was the most surprised; the owner when he received his half-crown plus trousers, or the traveller when he awoke to find he had no trousers to wear.

*   *   *

THE NUNNYWUTCH. When the parish Rector, visiting an ailing woman, asked about her health, she said: "I be better, but I do feel all of a nunnywutch." Not understanding the meaning of the word the Rector consulted "Old John", an authority on local matters "Well, sir." said John, "nunnywutch be one of them words what us poor folks do use that ain't got no meanin'."

S.G.B. in The Middle Watch

THE SLAUGHTER IN THE COUNTRY

Recently I received a letter from a farmer to say he had picked up pheasants and hundreds of small birds that had been destroyed by eating dressed spring corn, and today I read that at least 5,000 bullfinches had been shot and trapped in five years in one small area.

Being a life-long lover of birds I am much concerned about their well-being—as are others—but I fully realise that those who get their living from the land desire to improve their crops.

Surely some better method than the present one can be found, and one that will not endanger the lives of wild creatures.

The Wild Birds Protection Acts makes it illegal to shoot certain birds on the list, but it is unfortunate that there is no punishment for those who are guilty of poisoning them.

In 1952—when the Agriculture Bill (Poisonous Substances) was being debated in the House of Commons, a Member of Parliament stated that within a day or two of the spraying of 46 acres of brussels sprouts with organo-phosphorous insecticide there was a death roll of 175 animals.

Of these 158 were birds, including 10 pheasants and 19 partridges, and the other victims of this poison were rabbits, hares, rats, mice, a squirrel and a stoat.

Thousands of terns, swallows, and grebes, were slaughtered to supply the great demand for feather adornment in women's hats; greenfinches were sold in great numbers in paper bags in London for a halfpenny each; one man in Lancashire caught 95 dozen skylarks in a fortnight; sparrows and starlings were caught in thousands for shooting matches;

When there was craze for stuffed birds, kingfishers, bullfinches, and other birds were used for this purpose, and there was a ready market for the feathers, which anglers used for tying flies.

Nightingales were captured in great quantities, a salad of their tongues being considered a great delicacy, and in a recently published book the writer states that he caught and sold thousands of goldfinches.

The present terrible destruction of wild creatures by the indiscriminate use of lethal chemicals, and the squirting of poisons around the countryside, is a tragedy, and it is to be hoped that the scientific investigations now being carried out will result in the elimination of the chemicals responsible.

*   *   *

A HOLE FULL OF RABBITS

Many shooting men who own their estates can afford the cost of gamekeepers and beaters to provide them with their sport. Others join a syndicate, and farmers and friends form shooting parties to take part.

But it is doubtful if any of them get more satisfaction than one who has what is commonly called a rough shoot and is limited to week-end shooting especially one who has a knowledge of the habits of wild creatures.

The latter is most important as it will enable any shooting man to approach fur or feather with every chance of getting within reasonable distance of his object.

One great asset is to have a well trained and obedient dog; one that is not is better left at home.

I think the average shooting man gets far more pleasure from watching a dog at work than anything else and a good gundog will certainly find the game for him to shoot, and retrieve it from most inacessible places.

No genuine sportsman is concerned with the size of the "bag", rather is it the quality of the shooting and the manner in which it is obtained.

To get the best results care should be taken in approaching an object quietly and against the wind and avoid talking—the latter can be heard by all wild creatures as a danger signal at a considerable distance.

An old squire near Gloucester made it a condition that his guests were to talk only before and after shooting took place; it may have been considered as unsociable, but it was a wise precaution.

One nuisance in the field is a yapping dog that disturbs everything in the neighbourhood, yet my partner had one of this type which proved useful in an unexpected manner

While I stood at the top of a wooded slope he worked the dog from the bottom towards me, and the noise made by the animal, resembling that of a pack of hounds in full cry, was very effective.

SCORES OF RABBITS SCUTTLED PAST ME—TOO CLOSE TO SHOOT—AND I NOTICED SEVERAL DISAPPEAR INTO A HOLE. AFTER THE WOOD HAD BEEN CLEARED I WENT TO THIS HOLE AND PULLED OUT NINE RABBITS THAT WERE PACKED TIGHT IN A CUL-DE-SAC.

Two friends and myself were invited to clear up the rabbits in a big wood on hilly ground near Berkeley and on our arrival we were pleased to hear that the owner was going to send us a jar of cider to quench the thirst at lunchtime.

"Parking" our food near a large oak tree we then set forth through very thick undergrowth of brambles and bracken on a very hot day, and after spending four hours tearing through this jungle we returned to the starting point with a tremendous thirst.

Great was our consternation and disappointment that the promised jar had not arrived, and there was not a drop of water to be found in the neighbourhood.

I sat down on a mound of heaped-up leaves in disgust, and as I did so my foot came in contact with something solid. Curious to see what it was some of the leaves were removed and I discovered to my great joy—three pint-sized bottles of beer!!

Never was a drink so welcome, and we thanked dame fortune for coming to the rescue of three very thirsty men.

It was some considerable time afterwards we ascertained that a shooting party had been there the previous week; they had placed them in this place for their own use but were not able to locate them when needed.

*   *   *

WHEN CONCERTS IN THE VILLAGE HALL MEANT SOMETHING

Long before the days when people could sit in their homes and listen to entertainment provided by radio and television they used to to fill the village halls and other places and enjoy variety concerts provided by enthusiastic amateurs from Gloucester.

So great was their anticipation of these events that country folk would walk or cycle for miles, and on one occasion, when I went with a party to that outlandish hamlet of Syde, one farmer told me that he had ridden his horse 12 miles to see the show.

And this was in very bad weather in the winter, when the snow lay deep and crisp, but very uneven.
This concert was held in a barn and an electric cable was run from a near-by house to provide the lighting.

The stage consisted of planks of wood placed loosely on the top of empty boxes, and during a dance, one of the performers pirouetted across the stage, but getting too near the end of one of the planks her weight caused the other end to fly up and give her a resounding smack on the side of the head!

Though it was not intended to be a comedy dance the incident was much appreciated.

I was one of a party of six who made a journey to a village to give a performance at a local hall, and when we arrived there was a large crowd gathered near the entrance.

Was our visit so popular that the hall was already filled, and that those people outside were unable to gain admission?

Rather presumptuously, perhaps, these were our first thoughts, but we were to receive a shock.

The person responsible for the organisation of the concert was full of apologies, stating that the man in charge of the hall had gone to Gloucester to see a film, and had taken the key of the hall with him. So we went back home.

On another ocasion we travelled to Birdlip to give a show there, but instead of a crowd waiting to go into the hall there was not a single person in sight!

On making enquiries it was ascertained that no hall had been booked or concert advertised, and there was no one in the locality who knew anything about it.

Some of my happiest moments were with the Toc H. Concert Party, visiting many villages around the district to get funds to provide poor children with holidays in a camp at Cirencester.

The Rev. "Tubby" Clayton, the originator of Toc H. in France during World War 1 visited us on two occasions and we had some very happy times in his company.

The late Norman James was the driving force behind our enterprise, playing the piano, painting the scenery, providing the lights, and doing all the work essential to make the party a success.

I was engaged to provide some entertainment after a dinner given by masters of foxhounds to farmers and followers of hounds. There were about 200 present, and we had just started on the soup when the electricity system failed and the room was plunged into darkness.

Despite the sounding of many hunting horns and the shouts of "Tally Ho" the staff at the hotel were unable to find the cause of the trouble, and the dinner had to be abandoned.

When I once went to a country hotel to "tell the tale" to a dinner party there I found 'the room was very long and narrow, with a small platform at one end.

This was ideal, but when I saw two clergymen seated at the far end of the room it occurred to me that it might be necessary to put a blue pencil through some of my stories.

Being anxious not to embarrass these gentlemen I sought the opinion of the organiser of the dinner and concert, and he said: "You don't want to worry about the kind of stories you tell, for both of them are slightly deaf."

He added that one of them was the local vicar and the other a Roman Catholic priest.

Imagine, therfore, my surprise when getting on the platform to find that these two gentlemen had vacated their seats at the far end of the room and were now sitting in the front row about two yards away from me.

Their hearing may have been impaired, but to make sure they did not miss a word they both cupped their ears with their hands. It was a very awkward moment for me, for now I had to think quickly and try to remember some stories about clergymen that would not give offence.

*   *   *

THE DAY THE MATCH ENDED IN A FIGHT

In addition to earning a living, a lifetime's interest in birds and animals of the countryside, playing parts for nearly 40 years in the operatic and dramatic society, it has been possible to devote some time to sporting activities.

And now that I am in retirement I often wonder, when reading of some of the modern youths complaining they have nothing to do except sit in a coffee bar and listen to the alleged music coming from a juke box, how I found time to take part in such a wide variety of sport, and why I became interested in it.

Nothing of a sporting nature was ever taught at school, but perhaps it was here that the first seed was sown. Although I was a big boy other boys' used to knock me about, but I couldn't hit back because my parents held the view that if I was hit the proper thing to do was to 'offer the other cheek.'

A good principle no doubt, but my young mind rebelled against this, and unknown to them I joined a boxing club to learn something about the art of self-defence.

This, to my mind, was one of the best things I ever did, and although many may not agree with boxing the hard knocks I received gave me the self assurance that was needed.

Since then I have been in a boxing booth and sparred with the proprietor, got a medal for winning a contest at Gloucester Baths, and was twice runner-up in the finals of contests during World War 1 when serving in the 1/5th Gloucester's at Chelmsford, but apart from this I have never had a fight with anyone.

One of the days at Chelmsford I shall always remember; the hardest day's work I ever did. Before one of the boxing competitions our company did an hour's physical 'jerks,' including a three-mile run, in the early morning, and then a 22-mile route march with full pack on a very wet day.

After this tiring journey it was my lot to meet three contestants in the evening, and all this for one shilling a day!

The following day, Sunday, we attended service at Chelmsford Cathedral, and when the choir sang 'Fight the good fight'. I looked at one of my opponents of the previous night (with two lovely black eyes) and wondered if he thought the hymn was appropriate for the occasion!

When the world heavy-weight champion, Jack Johnson, came to this country I had an opportunity of seeing him boxing at Plymouth, and have also seen most of our champions in action since then.

37

One of the most curious things I saw in the ring was during a contest between a Cockney with cauliflower ears and an American negro.

About mid-way through the fight they went into a clinch, and suddenly the Londoner yelled: "'E's biting my . . . . ear!!", and the darkie was promptly disqualified by the referee.

Fame and fortune came to many professional boxers, but one man I knew that became a champion and won a Lonsdale belt died in poverty.

I followed this man's career very closely, and it was a sad sight for me to see him on one occasion leaning against a boxing booth at Gloucester fair holding out his cap to collect a few coppers, and another time, when attending a swimming gala, seeing him pushed into the baths fully clothed, and again go round with his cap, collecting coins from people who considered this was a humorous item on the programme. Such is fame!

At an early age an athletic secretary thought I might make a good runner and entered my name for a sprint race. The starter fired his pistol and we were off to a good start, and as the opposition did not seem great it seemed an easy race to win, but when trying to increase the pace near the end the effort caused my shorts to slip down to the ankles, and this most undignified competitor arrived at the winning post after turning two complete somersaults!

Physical development in my early days was a fetish. Swinging a sledge hammer on the anvil for the blacksmith; punching the 'sponge' for the baker's dough. weight lifting, walking, etc., so when I was persuaded to join a rugby football team there was plenty of opportunity to keep fit.

In trying to recall the thrills experienced in many pursuits in life it is a little difficult to single out any particular one, but perhaps the first should have pride of place. After playing rugby football with juniors it was a great thrill to receive a postcard from the Plymouth R.F.C. Secretary notifying me that I had been selected to play fro this first-class team in 1910.

After the Australians had toured this country they gave our club their mascot — a wallaby — and it created much interest with the spectators when it was paraded around the ground (on a lead) before the commencement of a game.

After moving to Bristol my debut for this team on the old county ground was a very inglorious one against the Gloucester RFC, trying to kick four penalty goals and missing the lot!

Although relegated to the second team the following week I regained a place in the first fifteen by a strange twist of fate. It was arranged that the second fifteen should play their game—against the Gloucester Regiment at Horfield — at 1.30, to give us an opportunity of watching the first team play Newport.

At the conclusion of our game we travelled back to the county ground, and then I was told that as the first team were a man short it was necessary for me to play in this match.

TWO MATCHES IN THE FORWARD LINE IN ONE AFTER—NOON WAS PRETTY TOUGH GOING!

One game against Cardiff at Cardiff Arms Park is memorable for a chapter of accidents. The fact that I lost a tooth when charging down a free kick is of no importance, but there were four men carried off that day on stretchers, three with injuries caused in vigorous play and the other by an accident which could not have been foreseen.

After our team had scored a try the player, trying to convert this, kicked the ball with such force that the cross bar was disloged and fell on a Cardiff man standing underneath, to render him unconscious and be carried off the field.

On one occasion I was a spectator at a match between two village teams who were deadly rivals. Before the game commenced one could feel the atmosphere among the spectators, and judging by the remarks overheard this was going to be no ordinary match.

From the beginning of the game there was trouble, the referee continually blowing his whistle for infringements and warning the players.

Then fighting broke out among the players and this in turn spread to the spectators, so much that the referee had no alternative but to order both teams off the field,—within ten minutes of the start!

AS A FORESTER SAID TO ME AFTERWARDS: "THERE WAS ZUMMUT GWAIN ON, I'LL TELL THA."

Many years ago that great Lydney enthusiast, Supt. Shelswell, told me an amusing story regarding a game his team played in Devon. One of the Lydney forwards — a short sturdy man — was marking a very tall opponent in the line-out, one who had a greater chance of getting the ball when thrown in from touch.

As the ball was thrown in the Lydney player made sure of getting his man with a good solid tackle, not caring whether his opponent had the ball or not. The latter was furious, and said in his best "Oxford" language: "What the hell are you doing? I haven't got the ball!" "No', said the Forester, "but thee's look a likely bloke to 'ave'n!".

As my Rugby club was without a fixture one week a friend of mine asked me to play full-back with him in an Association game my only knowledge of this game being gained as a goal-keeper for a small village club.

With great apprehension I accepted the invitation, but to become eligible to play it was necessary to sign a form as it was a minor league match.

Nothing very exciting happened during the game, and within a minute of full-time no goals had been scored, but then a foolish blunder I made caused the defeat of our team — the only one of the season!

One of our opponents kicked the ball high in the air towards me, and in true Rugby style I caught it and made a "mark" right in the penalty area! Though my eyes were too full of tears to see the man taking the kick my ears were open wide enough to hear the cheers from our opponents as the ball crashed into the net and the whistle blew for "time"!

*   *   *

THE CHARACTER AT THE VILLAGE INN

One of the likely places to find a "character" is in a village inn, and when passing an inn recently in Gloucestershire I remembered meeting an extremely interesting character there many years ago.

He was alleged to have been the vicar of a parish at one time, but now he was trying to earn a living by travelling around the countryside and selling cattle conditioning powders to farmers.

He guaranteed these would "cure all disorders consequent upon the reduced state of the nervous system."

When entering this inn I saw him sitting at a table enjoying a double whiskey, and in between sips entertaining the customers with stories regarding his previous life.

He was a most jovial man, and his laughter, added to that of his audience, really rocked the rafters.

Even if some of the stories contained only a grain of truth they were told with such enthusiasm that we listeners could have been excused for believing them.

Before taking a service he told us it was his custom to have a few drops of whisky. On one occasion the Bishop of his diocese was present at a morning service when our storyteller preached the sermon.

At the conclusion of the service the Bishop said to him: "Mr. Blank, I cannot understand how you can partake of strong drink and then go into the pulpit and preach a sermon."

"My dear Bishop," he replied, "I don't see how anyone could possibly preach a good sermon without having a drop of whisky!"

Mr Blank's parish extended over a wide area, and many of the people in it lived in rather squalid surroundings. While he was in bed one night he received a message that one of his women parishioners was extremely ill and would like to see him immediately.

The weather had been very bad for several days, and the journey to her house through deep snow was only made with great difficulty.

On arrival at her bedside he sat nearby and gave her some words of comfort, and then added: "What you need to put you right is some good neat whisky."

"Oh sir," she said, "I've never had any intoxicating liquor in my life, and I wouldn't have any now even if it would save my life."

40

"Don Alhambra" in "The Gondoliers"   *Last appearance in 1954*

Mr. Blank told us that from his position on a chair he had seen a partly filled bottle of brandy under the pillow on the bed!

"I returned to my home he said, "and had a couple of glasses of rum, then jumped into bed and cursed that old reprobate for calling me out on such a filthy night."

Some weeks later he received another urgent call, also very late at night, to go to the home of a man alleged to have been strangled in the room he occupied at the top of a tenement house in a slum area.

When he arrived at the house he saw a woman, the widow, but then unknown to him, and asked her to direct him to the room, and quite casually she said to him: "You'll find him up there on the third floor."

He ascended the stairs and found the room but when he saw that the man was gone beyond his aid he decided to leave the place. Just as he began the descent he encountered a man—a detective coming up to make an investigation. "What are you doing here?" asked the police officer.

He tried to explain who he was, but as he had left home hurriedly in some old clothes, and was unable to produce any evidence of his identification, the officer became suspicious and took him to the local police station.

When enquiries had been made and the police were thoroughly satisfied he was allowed to go home, but he said: "I needed a few drops from the bottle to put me right after that uncomfortable experience.

*   *   *

IDENTIFICATION. One night a woman went to see a film at the local cinema, and on her returning home her husband said that he had killed six flies, three male and three female. When asked to explain how he could tell on sex from another he said: "Three were on the mirror and three were on the meat."

ROTATING THE CROPS ? A farmer saved up some money and bought six acres of land, planted on acre of peaches, then left one acre unplanted and planted an acre of cherry trees, another acre unplanted and then an acre of plums. When he was asked why he left so much space between the the fruit trees he replied: "Well I must have some room to spit out the stones."

CANDLE IN THE WINDOW. A Scotsman living in the remote part of the Highlands, had been keeping a vigil at the bedside of his dying wife for several days. One evening he said: "Agnes, I must go out on business, but I will hurry back. Should you feel yourself slipping away while I'm gone, please blow out the candle.

THE OTTER THAT BEAT THE HUNT

Accepting an invitation to go to the meet of the Wye Valley Otter Hounds, I journeyed with the secretary in the sidecar of his motor-cycle to some water about four miles north of Tewkesbury, on a day when the rain never ceased.

After hunting had been in progress for some time the hounds picked up the scent of an otter and followed it to the roots of an old willow tree over-hanging a stream, and judging by the noise of the hounds at this point the animal was somewhere inside the trunk of the tree.

Before dislodging it the Master asked for a few of us to dam the narrow stream by standing in the water, which was about two feet deep; this he hoped would prevent the animal escaping.

An otter has to come to the surface for air as it cannot remain under water indefinitely. Air bubbles rising to the surface is an indication of its position, but with the rain descending on the water it was difficult to see these on this day.

And, incidentally, the animal could have pushed its nose underneath a floating twig to raise it sufficiently high enough to allow it to breathe, without any of us seeing it.

We stood in the water for nearly an hour, but although hounds were giving tongue to denote the presence of the animal it was never seen by anyone.

I was watching very intently for these air bubbles when suddenly the otter slipped between my legs with such force that I fell over backward backwards into the water.

This animal deserved to get away for the clever way it outwitted the heavy odds that were pitted against it, and perhaps I was the only one to feel happy that it did get away.

That was the end of the days hunting and we began our journey to wards home, hoping to make it quickly to enable us to have a change of clothing.

After proceeding along the road for a mile the engine "conked out," and despite every effort made it would not start again. The nearest garage was four miles away at Tewkesbury, and there was no alternative but to push the machine there to get it put in order.

The rain continued to fall heavily, and this, together with the perspiration oozing from our bodies, made us feel very uncomfortable, but when arriving at the garage we hoped that our difficulties would soon be over.

But after the mechanic had spent some time inspecting the machine he came to the conclusion that there was a fault in the magneto and a new one was necessary, but when asked to fit one he said he was sorry that he hadn't one in stock.

The thought of pushing the machine for another eleven miles to get home in such dreadful conditions was appalling.

However there was nothing else we could do but to continue our journey by shoving the darned thing along what seemed an unending road to Gloucester, and on arriving in the City must have looked like a couple of drowned rats!

When I met the owner of the vehicle a few days later he told me that there was nothing at all wrong with the magneto, and the cause of the trouble was very simple — a disconnected lead.

*   *   *

THEY GAVE HIM UP FOR DEAD, BUT

OLD HARRY CAME TO THE PARTY

It was customary for the landlord of the only public-house in the isolated village to provide a supper for his customers soon after Christmas each year, and for many years the special guests to be at the top of the table with him were three of the oldest inhabitants, Harry, Sam and Tom, three men who had all passed the allotted span of three score years and ten.

Invitations were again sent this year to this inseparable trio, and because of their advanced years transport would be provided for them. Sam and Tom readlily accepted the invitations, but as Harry— now in his eighty-sixth year — was seriously ill it was doubtful whether he would be able to attend.

An hour before the supper was due to begin the landlord received the grave news that the old man was not expected to last much longer; in fact, preliminary arrangements had already been made tor his funeral.

It can be imagined, therefore, what a great surprise it was to the company assembled when the old chap put in an appearance just before the meal started.

He was given a great reception on his arrival, and when the landlord asked him how he was feeling he said he had never felt better.

"When the doctor came and examined me," said Harry, "he said I'd got population of the 'eart, but I told'n I did'nt believe it. Then some of me relatives stood round me bed yesterday and I 'eard 'em talking about me funeral.

"One said they ought to 'ave two carriages, and when another of 'em said one carriage would be enough, cause of the expense. I jumped up in bed and told 'em that if one of 'em would get me trousers I'd walk.

"After they'd gone, and me 'ousekeeper gone to bed, I slipped downstairs and 'ad a good feed of the funeral am, and I felt better afterwards."

The first course of the meal consisted of mutton and caper-sauce with vegetables, and judging by the way old Harry set about the food it appeared that there was nothing wrong with his appetite.

I noticed, however, that he did not appear to be familiar with the capers, for these he pushed on the side of his plate. It may have reminded him of his days when tending sheep!

When the landlord asked if he would like a second helping of the meat he said he would, but added "Please don't cut it quite so close to the tail."

At the conclusion of the meal liquid refreshment was placed on the table and after a toast had been given to the landlord the 'old-timers' indulged in reminiscences.

All the trio drank their favourite beverage of cider, and being a very cold night they warmed this by putting a poker in the fire to get red hot before placing it in the cider; a little ginger being added to give it stimulus.

When old people gather together it is not unusual for them to recall incidents that occurred in the days of long ago, and on this night it was no exception.

Sam told us that when he was employed by a farmer and living in he was courting a girl in the village, and for "courting purposes" he was given a night off each week, but the farmer gave him two nights off each week if he attended church regularly.

Tom also amused the company by relating many incidents concerning his courting days, but he got the biggest laugh concerning his marriage when he said: "I didn't know 'er was bandy-legged till after the wedding!"

"Tom", said the landlord, "tell us that story about fishing you told me last week."

"All right," said Tom. "one day I took a gentle-man named Roe for a day's pike fishing in a lake, and 'e brought a farmer friend who 'ad a small terrier bitch.

"When a big pike was 'ooked 'e splashed about in the water a lot, and the dog got so excited that 'er jumped into the water after the fish.

"As 'er made a rush at'n the line broke. Then the pike chased the dog, and be damned if 'e didn't swallow 'er, every bit of her."

"Is that the end of the story?" said the landlord. "No," rplied Tom. "About three or four months later I was out with the same two gentlemen fishing the same water. The farmer 'ad the rod this time, and after fishing for 'alf an 'our darned if e' didn't 'ook the same fish!

"The fish tugged and tugged at the line, 'ard enough to break'n and it was only after a big fight 'e was landed. And what d'you think 'appened?'

"The pike swallowed the farmer," said Harry.

"No," said Tom, "the pike gave a big cough, and out of 'is mouth jumped the bitch followed by 'alf a dozen puppies."

*   *   *

COUNTRYSIDE REMINISCENCES

Where I now live flashes of lightning and thunderstorms appeared to have been above the average for July, and one terrific clap of thunder occurred — too close to feel comfortable — just at the time I was reading a book on the subject.

Few people are unawed during a severe thunderstorm, including myself, and many people who happen to be in the countryside seek shelter beneath a tree. I have done this on many occasions, choosing an oak tree if possible, as it is an old belief that this tree is sacred.

Incidentally, it is said that the bobbin at the end of a blind cord was shaped like an acorn to give people in a room protection against lightning, but, despite having several bobbins on his shop blinds a friend of mine in Gloucester — who was a tailor — found greater 'comfort' behind rolls of cloth in a dark room with a bottle of whisky.

The writer of the book I was reading claimed that trees with smooth bark suffer less damage than those with rough bark, and that usually the oak is more severely damaged than beech; water flows more easily down a smooth barked tree and renders it a better conductor.

I was very pleased to see the photograph of a tit's nest made in a letter-box at Dymock, and to note the kindness of the postal authorities who put a notice on the box 'Temporarily out of use except by nesting tit.'

Many tits have made use of letter-boxes for nesting purposes, but the nests I found of a great tit and blue tit touching each other in a small nesting-box was somewhat unusual. Bird's nests of robins and wrens I have discovered in hedgerows close together, but never anything like these of the tits in such close proximity.

It occurred to me that the birds might sit comfortably and hatch the eggs without any difficulty, but when the young ones were strong enough to get out of their nests, and probably return to the wrong one, would the parents have a problem in knowing which to feed ?

Here are a few oddities that I have taken from my scrap-book of memories.

Over 50 years ago one of the hind legs of a cow was broken just after delivering a calf, and she was able to walk after a veterinary surgeon fitted her with a wooden leg.

Blackbirds made a nest and reared their young behind a shelf of

"Dear Friends; Remember Me?"

bottles in the bar of a public-house, and another pair built their nest between the front wheels of two stolen bicycles awaiting collection at a police-station.

It is not only the wild creatures that do, what appears to human beings, strange things; domestic animals often act in a similar manner. Animals giving milk and allowing animals other than their own kind to suck them may seem odd, but this did occur when a calf took milk from a mare; a pig from a cow; and a goat, looking round and seeing a lamb helping itself at the 'milk bar' made no attempt to discourage the intruder.

May I put a question to readers. How many of you have seen apples growing up the trunk of a tree ?

*   *   *

BATTLE OF WITS WITH RATS AND PIGEONS

Are the birds and mammals of the countryside a pest or a benefit to farmers ?

From observations over many years in the fields and woods studying wild-life and in talking to the farmers and others, it is my opinion that a large percentage of wild creatures do more good than harm.

But those I would place on my 'black list' are rats, rabbits, wood-pigeons and grey squirrels.

Rats are the worst of our four-footed pests for they do enormous damage to food supplies.

In addition they damage by boring and tunnelling underground, and before the coming of the combine harvester they played havoc with standing ricks of corn;

Some years ago a companion and myself went to the knacker's yard at Sandhurst, and after I had used a crowbar to get rats from underneath heaps of bones and other material two very excellent terriers destroyed 69 of the creatures in less than two hours.

Despite the day being Sunday the extermination of these undesirable animals was hailed with satisfaction, and an interesting thing about this adventure was that my companion — veterinary surgeon who was a Roman Catholic — would not make the journey until he had attended Mass!

Our effort was not comparable, however, with a man, who, with two dogs, killed 134 rats in a single night in the underground area of a coal mine.

After I had used a trap — the cage - type — for catching rats under a shed in my garden it was hung on a nail, six feet from the ground in a coalhouse.

It remained there untouched for about 10 years, yet despite the trap being covered in coal dust, and without any bait to tempt them, I was astonished to find three rats in it one morning.

Although I am an enthusiastic lover of birds I have never hesitated to shoot such ravenous feeders as wood-pigeons; of all our birds they are probably the most harmful to growers of crops of any kind.

There is a record of over a thousand grains of wheat being taken from a single pigeon's crop, and another of 163 peas.

Knowing that pigeons are fond of peas I set up a 'hide' in a field planted with them, just at the time peas were ripe. With woods on three sides of the field, and a clump of trees surrounded by a fence was ideal for seeing and shooting.

Hoping to get a good 'bag' I placed out decoys at the break of dawn, but, although hundreds of birds alighted in the woods not a single one came down to the peas!

When I walked away just before dusk it was with the feeling that there was much more to learn about these wary birds.

The grey squirrel — often called a 'tree rat' — is a menace, not only to agriculture but to owners of woodlands, gardeners and naturalists, for it eats crops, strips bark from trees, and eats eggs and the young of wild birds.

On numerous visits to Cirencester it was my custom to pull up near a wood and watch the destruction caused by these pests to a rick of wheat in a field adjoining, and the damage done had to be seen to be believed; these animals, therefore, deserve all the hard things that have been said about them.

There is a much-debated question whether rooks do more harm than good to the farmer, but it seems to me that as the rooks feed on grubs — which are fatal to crops — for about nine months in a year they are of incalculable service, even if they take in return some ears of corn while it is growing, or eat it when it is ripe.

When watching a man sowing seed from a machine in one field, and another one turning over the soil with a plough in an adjoining field, it was interesting to see that while scores of rooks followed behind the plough in search of wireworms, etc., not a bird appeared in the field where the seed was sown.

*   *   *

FROZEN WORDS. Two Arctic explorers were discussing some of their experiences. One said to the other: "It was so cold where we were that the candle froze, and we couldn't blow it out." "That's nothing" said his rival, "where we were the words came out of our mouths in pieces of ice, and we had to fry them to see what we were talking about'.

WHEN A COUNTRYMAN GOES TO WAR

A few months after war had been declared in 1914, Fred Hardacre and Bill Stubble, who worked on a farm in a remote Cotswold village, took some cattle to market at Andoversford, and, during the day saw a poster "Your King and country need you" and; being true patriots, they decided it was their duty to offer their services.

So, after making arrangements with their employer they duly attended the drill hall for registration.

Nearly everyone who joined the Army at the time was sure that the war would be ended by the following Christmas, and with this in mind Fred and Bill had no doubt that they would soon be back again in their village.

After they had signed on the dotted line it was necessary for them to have a medical examination, and being hardened by long toil on the land these volunteers had no reason to think they would fail to pass the test.

Bill did this without difficulty, but Fred despite being found 'sound in wind and limb' was rejected because of defective eyesight.

At the end of the room was hanging a board on which there were rows of letters in various sizes, and Fred was asked to read one line at a time; this he was unable to do.

When the doctor asked him if he could see any letters on the board Fred said: "What board, sir?" The doctor could have rejected him immediately, but knowing that the Army urgently needed men he decided on another test.

He went outside the room, and then returned with the lid of a large dustbin. Holding this up about 20 yards away from the man he then said: 'What is this?' For a few moments Fred looked at it, and then to the doctor's amazement he heard Fred say: "I can't quite make out if it be a 'alf-crown or a two shilling piece!"

In the circumstances Fred returned to the farm, and Bill joined the Army and was sent to Aldershot, and there was no doubt he was 'up from the country' when he arrived wearing breeches and leggings and a bowler hat, garments that he had to wear for several weeks owing to the shortage of uniforms.

With other recruits he went on parade the following morning, and from the outset it was aparent that there was one man in that company who would not make a good soldier — and that was Bill!

When a musketry instructor was explaining to him the parts of a rifle, and how to load and fire, it failed to register in Bill's head, for when he was asked: "What is a fine sight?" the answer was: "Two dinners on one plate."

During instruction in bayonet-fighting the NCO noticed that Bill was continually resting, and he shouted to him: "Come on, get on with it." Bill told him that he couldn't because he was to old. "How old are you?", he was asked. "Thirty", was the reply "Thirty ! ! !, the instructor roared "do you know that the Romans used to do exercises up to the age of sixty?" "Perhaps they did," said Bill, "but I ain't a Roman; I be a Wesleyan."

As there did not seem any possibility of making the recruit into an efficient soldier he was given the job of batman for the colonel, and the rustic from the Cotswolds seemed more 'at home' in his new surroundings, but this lasted only for one day. The colonel, looking very perturbed, approached him in great haste and said: "Private Stubble, have you seen my baggage?" "Yes, sir," replied Bill, "she.'s just around the corner talking to the adjutant."

Eventually Bill was transferred to a Pioneer Battalion, and went to France, and when travelling on the boat proceeding along the river Seine he. said to the Captain: "'Ow fast do your ship travel, skipper?" "It used to travel at twenty knots, but now it only does nineteen," was the reply. And when Bill asked the reason for this he was told "Because somebody untied one."

A short time after Bill had arrived at the base camp he was sent to get some pudding from the cook-house, and when he returned without it he was confronted by an Orderly Officer who wanted to know what he had done with it, and Bill said he had eaten it. "Eaten it !" exclaimed the O.O., do you know that was the rations for eighteen men?" Poor bewildered Bill said he didn't know.

"And what have you done with the cloth?" the O.O. enquired. For a moment Bill was lost for a reply, then in a feeble voice said. "Was there a cloth on it sir?"

During the four years Bill spent at the base camp he failed to win any medals for distinguished conduct, and at the end of hostilities he returned to his old employer on the farm.

The first job he was given to do was to milk 26 cows and after he had milked several of them the 'boss' visited him and asked him how he was getting on. "All right," said Bill, "but don't you think I ought to have a bucket?"

*　　　*　　　*

GOOD FRYING. Talking during the service was very bad. The Vicar spode about it several times, but this had little effect. He was determined to stop it and arranged with the organist and choir to stop suddenly during a hymn, so that he could find out who it who it was. The plan worked well, for, in the silence that followed a lady's shrill voice was heard: "I always fry mine in lard." The Vicar said, "Now we know that the lady fries hers in lard, we will go on with the service."

BILL STUBBLE'S WEDDING – AND THE AFTERMATH

During the time Bill Stubble was in the army he found time to write to a young widow employed as a maid in the service of the squire of his native village in the Cotswolds.

Although these letters had to be written on odd pieces of paper and often without punctuation, there was no doubt about the sincerity of the contents.

Bill and Maggie had attended the same school, and from these days a great friendship had existed between them, so it can be imagined how happy was their meeting when Bill returned to the village after "doing his duty" as a soldier during the war.

In the quiet surroundings of their village they had ample opportunity of seeing each other again, and it was during the time they were sitting in a wood that Bill summoned up enough courage to pop the question. Maggie promptly acquiesced, and expressed a desire to get married as soon as possible..

News soon spreads with such a close community in a village, and when the banns were announced in church, it gave pleasure to all the inhabitants that the well-respected widow was to marry again, and many thought that Bill would be the ideal husband for her.

On the appointed day the happy couple stood before the parson and were duly wedded, and after the ceremony they accompanied him to the vestry to sign the register and pay the fee.

When Bill handed the fee of seven-an-sixpence to the parson he was astonished to have half-a-crown of this returned.

"Don't you usually charge people seven-an-six for being married at your church?" asked Bill.

"Yes," came the reply "but you married a widow: and I always allow a little for deterioration."

Let Bill describe the events that followed.

"We 'ad a wonderful reception in mother's house, and nearly everybody in the village seemed to be there. Maggie's mother had brought a big blancmange, but nobody knew 'ow to carve it,

"Fred 'Ardarce said: "Let's 'it in the middle and we'll all 'ave some.' I got mine all right down the middle of me back, but I didn't know it until I sat down.

"After the ceremony was over we packed out bags and went to Weston-super-Mare for our 'oneymoon. As it 'appened to be in the middle of the summer it was difficult to find accommodation but after walking about for two hours, we come on a place called 'The Haven,' and the landlady 'took us in' just before dark.

"After a wash and a good meal we 'ad a talk with other folk in the 'ouse until 'twas time to go to bed, and what a disappointment

Flitch Trial at Gloucester Guildhall

we 'ad when we got into the bedroom! There was a bed there all right, but 'twas only a single 'un.

"So far as I was concerned this was good enough, but I felt sorry for Maggie as 'er 'ad to sleep on the floor all night.

"Next day we left, and then 'ad a bit of luck in finding a boarding 'ouse where there was a nice comfortable double bed.

"That night Maggie lay with 'er 'ead on my ribs, and when 'er woke up in the morning 'er 'ad got a permanent wave in 'er 'air!

"After a swim we walked along the sands and watched a chap doing some conjuring, and 'e come up to I and said: 'You'd be surprised if I pulled a live rabbit out of your pocket, wouldn't you?' I told him I would. 'Why?' 'e asked. ''Cause I've got a live ferret in there,' I said.

"These sort of chaps thinks 'cause we come from the country we be daft, but something I saw in this town made I think that some of the people there 'aint so clever.

"When we got back to the boarding-'ouse I watched a bloke painting a door, and after 'e 'ad finished it 'e drove a lot of tin-tacks into it so I asked 'un what 'e did that for, and 'e said: 'To keep the paint from falling off.' It 'ad never occurred to I that this was the proper thing to do.

"The next day 'is foreman told 'un to dig a 'ole in the ground and after 'e did this 'e 'ad orders to fill it in again, and there was a great 'eap of soil left over.

"When I saw the man 'e was puzzled, and asked I 'ow to get the soil back into the 'ole again.

"After giving this careful thought, I said: 'There is only one thing you can do—you'll 'ave to dig the 'ole a bit deeper.''

After a very enjoyable week at the seaside the happy couple returned to their village cottage, and during their married life Maggie's only complaint was that she had to awaken Bill three times every morning, just for the pleasure he received when told it was not time to get up !

*   *   *

PROPER SERVICE. A girl who was visiting an old-fashioned country home feared that her brief silk pyjamas might shock the elderly servants, so she always put them away each morning before going down to breakfast. One morning during breakfast, she remembered that that she had not put them away. She hurried back, but the maid had got there first - she looked around but there were no pyjamas. She had a shock when the maid said: "If you are looking for the pyjamas, Miss, I've put them back in the young gentleman's room."

CAGE ME A CANARY

Janet and I live in a beautiful flat, three climbs up, surrounded by sunflowers and roosters on the washtub. It is rather lonesome, something like the A sharp at the left-hand end of the piano keyboard.

"Gerald!" said my life partner, stirring the kitchen fire with the muzzle end of the bellows, "Mr. Jacobs (a Scotsman from Palestine) is going to give me such a dinky little canary and I want you to make a cage for it."

I had never attempted to make a cage in my life, and, had I been of a hopeless nature, the mere suggestion of it might have had a very depressing effect.

"You know how to make a cage, don't you?" said she. I gave her a reassuring wink.

In fact, I knew so little about it that I didn't think it safe to converse more fluently than by winks.

Ever since I robbed a nest in my younger days the longing to keep birds had seized me. There was some hidden mystery about it, and mysteries force a man to think, and injure his health.

Glowing accounts had appeared in various journals on birds and of the wealth to be obtained in breeding them. We needed to increase our income, and Janet did her share by giving music lessons, she being a first-class disturber of the piano.

When we had finished breakfast, Janet, playing with her toothpick, said to me: "Will you make a cage for me dear?"

"By the piper that played before Beelzebub, I will!" said I. I heard her breathe hard. like a horse when the saddle is taken off. She looked as pleased as a kitten with its first mouse.

It is said that the less a man knows about anything the more willingly he engages to do it, and I had confidence in myself from the lowest button of my waistcoat upwards.

My experience as a corkscrew straightener stook me in good stead. There was no difficulty in getting plenty of wire and solder for I had a friend who was a lineman in the Post Office.

The first brilliant discovery I made was that I hadn't any tools and one must have tools. "Janet," says I, "go and borrow some pliers and a rule; then slip round to Ben Johnson's with my kind regards and say that I hope his boil is better, and will he lend me his soldering iron."

While she was gone I thought I would put a nail in the wall where we should hang our treasure, so, standing on a chair, placed at an awkward angle, and holding the nail in postion with my left hand, I aimed a blow at it with the hammer, smashed my thumb, dropped the hammer on the baby and slid down on to the piano; a really fine musical effect being produced!

At that moment the Goddess of Grub returned with the necessary implements. She screamed when she saw blood. "You're the awkwardest man I ever saw," she said. It was an easy remark, and 99 per cent. of women would have said the same thing.

I picked myself up and tied up the wound in silence, and then renewed my effort with zeal somewhat abated.

At the next attempt the nail went clean through the plaster, and half the hammer with it, my nose hitting the wall with such a thud that an earthquake must have been registered at the Observatory.

My temper rose by steady and sure degrees, and when Janet sympathised with me I said: "Sympathy without relief is like mustard without beef."

A passing policeman stopped below, with one ear upturned, and tried to analyse the noise. Said he: "'Tis the queer chap on the top flat, and his missis at it again. Married folks they be, and few pleasures they get." Then he walked away to blow the froth off a pint.

Using the lid of a biscuit tin for the foundation a real attempt was made to construct the cage. It is said that Dame Fortune calls on each of us in our lifetime, but her daughter, Miss Fortune, called on us this particular day.

Nothing went right. Hot solder dropped on my fingers, and the soldering iron fell out of the fire and burnt the smelling end of the cat. Then a knife slipped and cut my knuckles with a ferocity almost human. I went into the back kitchen to think, and Janet went upstairs to weep, and then the door bell rang. I answered it to see a small boy standing there with a brown paper parcel under his arm. He said his father—Mr. Jacobs—was very sorry that the promised canary had died, and he had sent something else.

The "something else" was a rabbit which looked like a cross between an Angora and box of lemons!

Now I have the problem of making a rabbit hutch!!

*   *   *

THE CHEEK OF "BOUNCER"

There are many men who have made Gloucester famous by their achievements, and their names have been recorded in the history books, but so far as I am aware no place has been found for one of the City's inhabitants known to a vast number of local people as "Bouncer'"

I knew him for many years during my residence in Gloucester as one who hated hard work of any description, but he had a way of seizing on a situation to get money in case of necessity.

56

One Sunday evening when he was walking along the London-rd. he met a friend. He was invited to go to a public-house and have a drink, but he said that he had no money.

"That's all right," said the friend, "I've got enough for a couple of pints",,and they walked towards the inn on a very dark and stormy night.

Before they had gone 300 yards "Bouncer" stepped off the pavement, and then held up his hand and stopped a motorist proceeding towards the City.

When the driver alighted and asked the reason for this "Bouncer" told him that his number plates were covered in mud, and advised him to clean them as the police were stopping and checking all cars near the George-st. Post Office.

The driver was most thankful for this timely warning, and to show his gratitude put two half-crowns in the hand of his benefactor. What the driver thought when he discovered there were no police on duty at George-st. can be left to the imagination!

Getting money in this easy way was one of "Bouncer's" specialities, but he was also capable of enjoying a "joke" at the expense of someone else.

Late one winter's night he was standing near the Cross when an elderly gentleman pulled up his car, leaving it near the kerb while he went to the New Inn for a drink. A few minutes later a rough looking tramp appeared in Westgate-st. and "Bouncer" in his best "Oxford" language asked him if he would like to earn a shilling. Of course he would!

"Just sit in my car, and wrap a rug round yourself to keep warm," said "Bouncer", then he went to hide in a door-way.

When the owner returned pandemonium broke out. The tramp refused to move because he had been promised a shilling for looking after the car, and despite the owner's efforts to eject him forcibly he failed.

Eventually he decided to give the old tramp the shilling and get rid of him, much to the enjoyment of "Bouncer" peering from his hiding place.

For a very short time this notorious character was employed by builder, and one day he was given a job to do in Northgate-st.

It meant getting up a ladder—which he hated—and putting some cement on to fill up a few cracks. He mixed the cement on the ground, and then left to visit a nearby public-house.

Soon afterwards the foreman appeared on the site, and waited there for two hours. When "Bouncer" appeared, limping very badly, he was asked: "Where have you been ?"

Presumably in great pain, he replied: "When I went up the ladder two kids pinched my cement and I've been all the morning chasing 'em round St. Catherine's Meadow!"

"Well," said the foreman, "you're sacked, and I hope it won't be too painful for you to walk home."

"Bouncer" possessed the gift of the gab to a marked degree, and he knew how easy it was to bluff the gullible public. He had a plausible tongue and a slick line of patter and as a salesman he could have sold mothballs in a nudist colony.

On one occasion he visited a market without any money, but with his own brand of ingenuity he "touched" someone for a shilling.

With this he bought some flour and a quantity of small envelopes, and after putting a small portion of the flour in each envelope he sealed them up and then took up a stand in the corner of the market.

The crowds soon gathered around to hear him talk about his wonderful cure for corns. The ingredients, he said, were obtained form the tall trees in Africa at great personal risk by his friends and then sent to him.

He quoted Byron as saying 'Sometimes the largest things are found in the smallest proportions,' and then pointed out how truly the saying applied to his corn cure.

"The lady or gentleman who buys this little lot will come up and shake me by the hand," he said.

Similar patter continued for a few minutes, and then he announced that the price was "not two and sixpence over a mahogany counter or three half-pence for Government stamps; Just sixpence to advertise my firm."

The audience swallowed the "bait" and within five minutes bought the whole of his stock. The taking of thirty shillings for an outlay of one shilling was not bad business.

I saw him in Gloucester Market on one occasion—he dared not appear at any one place more than once—and this time he displayed on a table the biggest bone obtainable from a bullock and the heads cut from three codfish.

Surrounding these was an assortment of round objects, cut with a mould, about the size, and a little thicker than a half-crown.

They were coloured red, green, blue and yellow, and the customer had the choice of either at a cost of threepence each.

These objects were guaranteed to keep flies away from any room and as it was a very hot day and no flies went near the bone and fish this seemed to be true.

I, therefore, became on of the 'mugs' that bought some. Later I tried them at home and found them to be useless.

Some time after this I discovered that the objects had been made from tallow candles and coloured with different kinds of dyes. The reason no flies were attracted by the bone and fish in the market was that these articles had previously been dipped in paraffin. Incidentally there were no flies on "Bouncer."

At one time "Bouncer" did a certain amount of professional boxing around the district, but if things were going against him he would go down from the slightest punch and remain there for the

Playing Bowls at Southsea (on tour) with Gloucestershire team

count of ten, the result being that the public refused to attend shows if he was on the programme.

His manager had a "brainwave" and took him to a distant part of the country where he was not known. There he appeared, with other boxers belonging to the booth, and was introduced as "The Zulu Kid."

He wore shoes and long trousers but from the waist upwards the whole of his skin had been covered with a black substance.

As it was a dark night, and the only light provided came from the old hissing oil lamps, the crowd standing around accepted him as a genuine coloured man—which he was.

People crowded into the booth to see the "negro" have a scrap. The first two rounds were uneventful, but during the third round the audience had a shock!

Owing to the excessive heat caused by the packed audience and the overhanging lamps the untrained Zulu Kid perspired very freely so much so that it ran down his face and body to remove his black covering and reveal a white skin.

Immediately the crowed realised the deception one man seized the bucket of water near the corner of the ring and threw it over the "darkie" and then, because the owner of the booth would not return their admission money, they wrecked the tent.

One amusing episode in the life of "Bouncer" I remember was on the occasion he set out for the day to go fishing with a local fishmonger.

They were supposed to go to the Leadon, but the refreshment in a public house was so much to their liking that they never reached this stretch of water.

"Bouncer" had promised to bring his wife some fish so when he arrived back in Gloucester he told his pal that he could not go home without some. "That's all right," said his pal, "give me your basket and I'll go into the shop and put some in for you."

He did this and "Bouncer" went home feeling very pleased. On his arrival his wife's words were: "If you've got some fish I'll cook it for your supper."

"You'll find some in the basket," said her husband. And she did. Wrapped in several pieces of newspaper was—a tin of sardines!

*   *   *

ANCIENT LETTERING. A collector of old furniture was bargaining for an old chair. "It's Queen Anne, sir, I tell you," said the vendor. "It may be, but how do you know it is?" "Well, you see these letters, sir - 'Q.A.' they stand for Queen Anne." "If they stand for Queen Anne, " retorted the Collector, "I've got a door at home that dates back to William the Conqueror !"

QUEER PLACES FOR A NEST

I have found a robin's nest in a cast-off boot in a bed of nettles, but one that surprised me was made in a shopping basket attached to the front of a woman's bicycle.

The skull of a horse lying in the corner of a farmyard was another place chosen by a pair of robins to rear a family.

The members of the tit family choose sites in inverted flower pots, letter - boxes, disused pumps, and one nest I found in a piece of down-pipe resting against a shed in a builder's yard. It made me wonder how it was possible for the young — four feet down — to get out!

Wrens, too, will nest in unusual places, and I have found them in a ball of twine and a broccoli plant, but perhaps my best 'find' was in the carcase of a carrion crow hanging, with other dead birds, on a game-keeper's gibbet, parts of the nest being interwoven between the crow's wing feathers.

It is well-known that birds will return each year to the same nesting site swallows having done so for fourteen years to an electric light meter in the porch of a house.

Two years in succession swallows made their nests on a meat-hook hanging from a nail in the rafter of an outhouse, a photo-graph of which I have in my possession, and during the construction of these nests it must have been a very difficult task for the birds as the hook moved to and fro each time they alighted on it.

Swallows also made their nest in a barn at Maisemore, the doors of which were generally closed, and I watched them on several occasions make their only entrance and exit through a knot-hole in one of the doors.

There are three occasions I remember expending a lot of energy climbing trees to inspect some nests, but the rewards have been quite different from that expected.

After seeing a barn owl fly out of a hole at the top of a tree— during the breeding season— I climbed the tree to ascertain if it had been sitting on eggs. It was not possible to see any, so I put my hand down the hole. Suddenly there was a terrific commotion as another owl flew out and hit my face a resounding whack with its wings.

Ascending another tree to look at what appeared to be a nest— actually it was the drey of a squirrel—I was greatly surprised to find it occupied by a stoat.

When descending a pollarded withy tree—after looking at the nest of a mallard duck—I received an awful shock as a fox—minus its brush—went between my legs as it bolted from a hole at the bottom of the tree.

It is a good plan after finding a nest to see that none of the plants or foliage around it is broken, so that the locality is not revealed to human or other enemies.

THE LAST TRUMP

Dan Russell, the author of "Working Terriers," relates a good story in his book about badgers, and I am indebted to him for allowing me to use it.

In one of the loveliest villages in Gloucestershire some men decided to go badger-hunting. A watcher was first sent to a big earth in Small's Wood, and then the hunters were ready to start.

In order to make plenty of noise Arthur borrowed a bugle from the blacksmith, who played in the village band. The party broke up and the men set off, each on his appropriate beat.

Arthur made his way to the top of the hill which overlooked the village and there he blew long and loud upon his bugle; at least he produced a noise which could be heard a long way away on that quiet, moonlit night.

After his trumpet voluntary he walked along the top of the hill to an old tumulus which stood opposite Small's Wood where the men were to meet.

He stood on the tumulus mound and again he made the night hideous with his bugling.

Far away he could hear the other men as they beat through the woods; he made up his mind that the time had come to go down to meet them. He left the tumulus and crossed the road into the big field which lay about the wood.

And then, as he walked over that field, he saw a tall white shape gliding towards him. 'Who be you?' he asked, but there was no reply, just the white apparition gliding towards him in the moonlight.

He is a big man, and in those days he was famed as the strongest man for miles around, but this unearthly sight broke his nerve and he turned and ran for it.

Sobbing for breath he reached the stone wall which bordered the wood and sank down upon it exhausted.

And then something touched him on the shoulder and a voice said: 'Oh Lord, I am ready.' He looked up and recognised his pursuer as an old woman who lived in a near-by lonely cottage.

She had heard the bugle and thought it was the Angel Gabriel blowing the Last Trump. Clad only in her long white night-gown and her night cap she had come out to greet the herald of judgment.

The poor soul had been ailing for some time and the next day was taken to a place where she could be looked after.

*   *   *

CLOSE–UPS OF ANIMALS

An elderly friend of mine once told me that the best way to study wild life was "to observe without being observed."

Sometimes a place for concealment is not always available, but it is possible to get excellent opportunities for observation in the open by getting to know the habits of animals ascertaining which are alarmed by movement, and which by sound.

If care is made to advance against any prevailing wind it is a very easy matter to approach hares and rabbits in 'forms' without disturbing them.

It is not always possible to get a close-up of certain animals, but a method I have used with foxes, rabbits, stoats, and weazels, has been very successful.

All these creatures respond very readily to the squeal of a rabbit, and a good imitation of this can be made either by pursing the lips tightly and sucking inwardly, or by pressing the lips on the back of the hand to do so.

Some practice is essential to make the 'squeal' effective, but the effort will bring great rewards.

Many times I have taken cover and used this call to bring all these animals to within a few feet of my position, on one occasion calling a vixen away from a dog fox some two hundred yards away—a great opportunity to take a picture had I been a photographer.

Fierce fights among the wild creatures are continually going on, and it is not unusual to see one attacking another of its own kind that has met with an injury; twice I have seen a cock pheasant attack another that has been shot and was fluttering on the ground.

I learned a lot about wild life in the company of gamekeepers, I spent a good deal of time with them in the search for pheasants eggs during the breeding season.

It was during this time I saw a keeper give an exhibition of shooting that was remarkable.

As we walked near a hedgerow he, hardly checking his stride, bent down and caught a rabbit in a 'form' but before he could kill it another rabbit jumped up from the grass and ran away.

With his left hand he placed the live rabbit between his knees, then brought his gun to the shoulder and fired. The rabbit turned several somersaults before I picked it up—shot behind the ears; a good example of the co-operation between eye, hand, and mind.

From a place of observation I have seen a fox pick up a pheasant that had been shot and then proceed to bury it in the ground.

A stoat, performing its 'acrobatics' before seizing a rabbit has been seen by many, but once it was my good fortune to see this agile creature seize a rabbit and drag it across a field—the rabbit being still alive—and when it reached a tree several young stoats came out of a hole at the base and had a good feed from the meal the parent had provided.

Stoats are also fond of fowls eggs, and one I disturbed from a heap of straw in a barn provided the evidence by the number of empty shells there.

It has always puzzled me how stoats and weasels can so influence a rabbit into submission, but when I saw a weasel pursuing a hare it seemed ridiculous that the larger animal with its terrific speed could not use it to avoid its tiny pursuer; this problem, and many others, teaches us that there are things in nature we may never understand.

It is known that hedgehogs have a liking for milk, sometimes taking that which trickles from the overfull udders of resting cows, but one I saw with its head in a condensed milk tin must have been very grateful when I removed the tin from its head.

*   *   *

ALL IN A DAY ONE SUMMER

From a position in a wood I had been watching a tree creeper silently working its way up from the bottom of a tree in search of insects in the crevices of the bark, when my eye caught a movement on the ground — a sexton beetle in the act of burying a dead mouse.

It was interesting to see how it lowered the dead animal into a grave by first excavating the earth from underneath it, and then covering the body.

After the burial the beetle lays its eggs on the corpse, and when the young are born the dead mouse provides a plentiful supply of food for them.

Apart from the wild creatures killed by accident on the roads very few dead ones are seen in the countryside, and this I think can be accounted for by the number of animals which eat carrion, or dispose of them like the sexton beetle.

On leaving the wood I walked along a Cotswold stream, and then sat on an old tree stump to watch a wonderful display given by several dragonflies — sometimes known as the 'devil's darning needles.'

As they dashed from their positions on bushes to catch flying insects I noted their beautiful colouring and graceful forms as they swooped in the summer air, to alight again on the bushes to devour their prey.

It was the latter part of May, and my good fortune to be near a stream on one of the few days when a mayfly is on the wing; not many of which enjoy their brief freedom to the full.

It has many enemies from the time it acquiries its wings, birds destroying many, and trout rising to capture any that venture too near the surface of the water.

Anglers, too, also take advantage of this period to secure many of the fish, one man who owned the riparian rights taking several close to my resting place.

During a conversation with him I was invited to his house adjoining the stream, and there he cooked a brace of trout for me to enjoy one of the best meals I ever had, and to appreciate the good things of life.

He had travelled to many parts of Britain to cast a fly on the various rivers and streams, and he was no exception to other anglers when relating stories of the big fish that get away.

On being shown around his garden I noticed several beehives, and hanging outside the entrance to each was the silhouette of a cat cut from tin. I was told that they were to scare away tits.

These birds had been seen to settle on the alighting boards—during the winter particularly—and then tap on the boards with their beaks until the bees ventured into the open—perhaps out of curiosity—to be eaten by the birds.

After bidding my host farewell I again followed the path along the stream until my nose caught the smell of a field of beans in flower. As the gentle breeze wafted my way I was indeed thankful for one of my senses, for surely there is nothing in the countryside that smells so sweetly as this flower after a shower of rain and sunshine!

Just before dusk a jackdaw on some railings outside a cottage attracted my attention, the bird was hardly recognisable because it had lost most of its feathers.

Obviously it was a tame one for it greeted me with a 'hello' as I approached it, and when I made some enquiries about it at the cottage the owner said: "The darned old fool got all 'is feathers burnt off when 'e perched on the top of my oilstove when it was lighted'.

These are a few of the incidents in a day spent in the countryside, free to all who care to partake and enjoy the simple things in life.

*   *   *

OPEN PLAN. A Bishop (who shall be nameless) was in poor health , and having much travelling to do, took a lady nurse with him. Finding it sometimes difficult to get a bath in out of the way places, a rubber bath was included in the luggage. One day a friend asked him 'Are you aware that the nurse is using your bath?" The Bishop said he was not aware of that fact but will enquire into it. He then approached the nurse: "Am I correctly informed that you are using my bath." "Yes, my Lord," said the nurse. "Well, I don't mind your using it at all, but what I do object to is your using it behind my back," said the Bishop reproachfully.

NESTS WHERE YOU DON'T EXPECT THEM

We often hear of; or find for ourselves, the nests of birds in strange places—that is, in spots we should never suspect nests to be.

Many birds prefer the hedgerows in lanes with high banks, and ditches below the hedges where tall weeds and other herbage afford cover, while others build in most inaccessible places, such as a pair of rooks which contrived to lay the foundation of theirs on a weather-vane, and tits finding their way through a small hole and making their nest in the interior of a weather-cock, both of these being on top of a church spire.

Cuckoos will place their eggs in the nests of many kinds of birds, but how they managed to do so in the nest of a wren and in that of a house-martin under the eaves of a golf house, is a puzzle to all those who try to find out something about the mysteries of Nature. In the latter case the egg was never hatched as the nest was displaced by an over eager person.

Members of the tit family choose letter-boxes, street lamps inverted flower-pots, disused pumps, and many other places to build their nests, and the great tit and blue tit have been known to place theirs close together in a small box; nests of robins and wrens have also been found actually touching each other.

After many years of searching for nests one hopes to acquire a knowledge of the particular kind of surroundings any bird is likely to choose for a building site.

Even so birds have been known to choose unusual sites for many years, Gilbert White recording the nest of swallows in the handles of garden shears nearly two hundred years ago.

Starlings, which usually build their nests in holes in trees or under the roofs of buildings once made a nest in the deserted honeycomb of some bees in a tree.

New methods in agriculture and the encroachment of industries into the countryside have probably caused some birds to vary their habits in nesting, and the extensive spraying of trees and hedgrows has made it more difficult for them to obtain their usual building material.

A pair of chaffinches that made their nest in a shrubbery almost entirely of cotton-wool found in the grounds of a nearby hospital proved that birds, like all other wild creatures, can readily adapt themselves to circumstances.

It is well known that broody hens and birds will sit on sham eggs— I once saw a hen sitting on two old telephone insulators at Dursley— but when ducks laid two eggs in a nest at the bottom of a hedge a pair of blackbirds that took possession of them were confronted with the difficulty of covering them with breasts and wings; they solved the problem by hollowing out the bottom of the nest so that one egg was over the other!

Recently I saw an illustration when birds—black-birds—could not make up their minds in chosing a site for a nest.

Between the rungs of a ladder hanging on a wall outside a house they partly constructed nine nests before deciding to complete one, where the eggs were deposited and a brood reared.

*   *   *

TALL TALES IN THE "LOCAL"

"I gets 70 mouldiwarps (moles) and when I sends the skins to London all I get for 'em was a farthing a piece; downright robbery it was after all my hard work catching and skinning'em."

Tom was relating this story to two of his friends in the "local" where I met them. They were all old countrymen who talked about subjects like bats getting entangled in women's hair, rats carrying eggs between their forelegs, adders swallowing their young when danger threatens, and many other things that interest men who have spent a lifetime in the countryside.

I was very interested to hear about a method used by Sam for catching wild ducks, He was most emphatic in explaining that to be successful in catching any wild creature "you must use your 'ead and know something about their 'abits."

"You want to be a good swimmer to catch ducks," said Sam, "and the best time to do it is when the moon is up. Just before dark I get under cover of a bush down close to the edge of the pond, and stay there and watch the ducks drop on the water.

"When they've finished I take off me clothes and rub badger fat all over me body to keep out the cold.
"I ties a bag round me waist, and then put a thin piece of metal tubing, about 18 inches long, between me teeth, bent into shape so that one part be above me 'ead and I can breathe when I be under water.
"I get into the pond very quietly and swim under them ducks, then collars 'em by the legs and puts 'em in the bag."

Tom said he had never heard of ducks being caught like that and I agreed with him—but if ever he found the nest of a duck he used to take some of the eggs if she had not started to sit on them.

He contended that a duck could only count up to four, so as long as he kept the number below this she continued to lay and provide him with a feed!

Old Harry, a man of 84, minus most of his teeth and a bit thin on top, chuckled when he heard these stories.

"I can beat the lot of you." he said. "When I was a woodman I used to get a lot of rabbits out of some old hollow wooden logs that was lying about on the ground. These logs was burned, and when some of the trees was cut down I gets me an idea.

"The trees was lying on the ground, so I painted a black circle about a foot across on the sawn end of each trunk, to make it look like a hollow in the tree.

The rabbits used to go out into a field adjoining and about a fortnight after the trees 'ad been cut down I takes me two dogs into the field and looses 'em.

"As each rabbit got up one of the dogs chased 'un into the wood and, thinking the circle on the bottom of the tree was a hollow made a dive for it and broke its neck."

It would have been tactless of me to suggest that any of these stories were untrue, for I had enjoyed the company of this trio of old-timers in a reminiscent mood.

*   *   *

FOX TO RESCUE OF TRAPPED MATE

Wood Pigeons were destroying the crops of a land-owner near Newent, and he telephoned to say that he would be glad if I could spare the time to try to shoot them.

Several fowls had been killed by foxes, and the destruction of these would please him equally well.

Early the following day I placed myself just inside the edge of a wood, but not a pigeon came within range during the morning. At lunchtime it occurred to me that a move to another part of the wood might be advantageous.

Just as I was about to leave the sight of a vixen crossing the adjoining field made me decide to 'tarry awhile,' keeping an eye on the fox as she disappeared through a gap in the hedge some hundred yards away.

Ten minutes later a dog fox, presumably her mate, followed in exactly the same line he too going through the same part of the hedge.

Pigeons were not coming into the wood so I decided to creep under cover to a point as near as possible to the place where the foxes had made their exit from the field.

On arriving there I peered over the hedge and greatly to my astonishment, saw the two animals not 20 yards away.

Here was an opportunity to shoot at what can be described as a sitting target, but, however much the owner of the land wanted these animals destroyed, I couldn't have done it.

The hind leg of the vixen was caught in a rabbit snare, and I watched in amazement as the dog fox tore at the cord (which

68

held the wire to a wooden peg in the ground) until he had bitten it away and released his mate.

Wild creatures do readily adapt themselves to circumstances, but never did I expect to see such a practical demonstration.

MATERNAL INSTINCT OF A STOAT

The maternal instinct in wild creatures is very strong, and I have been thrilled on many occasions during my observations of their habits.

The following incident is a good illustration of the love a mother has for her offspring.

A gamekeeper friend of mine was walking around his 'beat' one evening—throwing corn from a sack to the pheasants he had reared —when he saw a stoat crossing a lane with several young ones trailing behind.

The mother succeeded in getting to the hedgerow but two shots from the keeper's gun destroyed the youngsters.

Thinking that he might be able to tempt the parent to come out from the hedgerow, he took cover behind a tree and imitated the 'squeal' of a rabbit, but the wily animal failed to respond to his call.

He therefore collected the young stoats and put them in a heap in a ditch, covering them over with the sack before going off to a distant field to close some hencoops.

Some 20 minutes later he returned and again tried the 'squeal,' but it was time wasted.

Imagine his surprise when picking up the sack to find that the old stoat had returned in his absence and taken away the young ones!!!

*   *   *

CLOSE—UP OF MAGPIES

Magpies are not easy birds to get a close look at, but I once had the luck to watch a pair nesting.

They had started to build in the top of a thorn hedge which adjoined a shed, where it was possible to look through an aperture and see these masterbuilders at work.

First the birds collected twigs and put a layer at the bottom, with mud and clay to bind them together, and then proceed to build upwards in this manner, leaving a hole just large enough to admit the bird's body at the side near the top of it.

A kind of roof was placed over it and then fenced around the

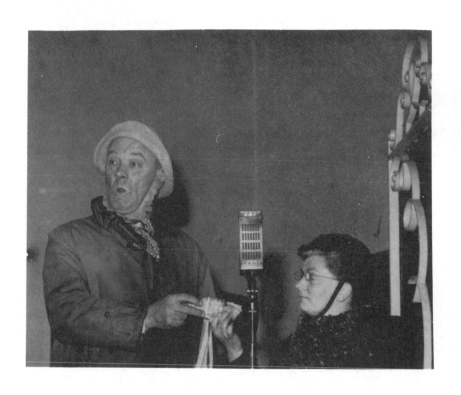

Claimants at the Flitch Trial, at Gloucester S.G.B. and a Lady Friend

outside with what seemed the sharpest thorns the birds could gather.

Anyone who has put a hand in the hole of the nest in search of eggs will have painful memories of the thorns encountered in the entrance!

The roof, or dome, surmounting the nest was, presumably for protection against any large bird of prey which might wish to force its way in, either to suck the eggs or take possession of it, for it would not be protection against rain.

I noticed that the sitting bird always had its face towards the doorway ready to escape at a moment's notice and it did this at the first alarm by dropping down perpendicularly several feet a habit it has to mislead its foe when wishing to get away.

Apart from the huge construction made by ravens the one made by magpies probably takes longer to build than any other, for this particular one took more than a fortnight to complete.

Although the magpie is one of the most conspicuous birds to be seen in the countryside, it is probably the wariest of the crow family never wanting close acquaintance with human beings.

Its colour is described as black and white but close observation reveals that it has a rich metallic green on its black feathers.

Its nature is to be ever on the move, going form place to place with a wavering, and what appears to be uncertain flight. Very alert, suspicious, and inquisitive, it has eyes and ears that are always open ready to detect a foe.

This so-called long-tailed pirate does, unfortunately, destroy many of the eggs of our song-birds and many owners of poultry have conclusive evidence of the damage done to the eggs of domestic fowls.

There are many legends regarding magpies, one being that, after the Crucifixion, while other birds prepared to show their grief, these birds would only put on half-mourning, and its punishment has been to wear it ever since, and that its name shall be associated with ideas of evil.

Many were the beliefs of the old country people who were superstitious. A hat would be doffed when a magpie was seen; men of Devon are alleged to have spit over the right shoulder three times and uttered an appropriate rhyme; but one farmer who thought the magpie was in league with the powers of evil was sure he could scare the birds away by cutting a cross upon the bark of a tree!

*   *   *

71

CROWS LIVE BY THEIR WITS

February is the month of the year when birds will be thinking of mating and building nests, and some of the first to be seen in these activities will be the familiar and most abundant members of the crow family, the rooks.

In many cases they like to nest near human habitation, and large colonies can be found in elm and other trees in land adjacent to the older houses around the countryside.

Trees in the vicinity of village churches often harbour many rooks and the cawing of the birds and ringing of church bells are welcomed by most parshioners.

Farmers differ in their opinions regarding their value or otherwise to agriculture, but as the birds' diet consists mostly of worms beetles slugs, insects etc., it can be reasonably assumed that this alone must benefit anyone with land under cultivation, although there is no doubt that rooks are liable to disturb some growing crops in their search for food.

Probably a rook has a more varied diet than any other bird, depending on the season of the year, but it is undoubtedly doing good when following the plough and devouring the many caterpillars, leather-jackets and wireworms which are exposed to view as the soil is overturned.

The countryside would not seem complete to me without the rooks during nesting time, and I have enjoyed many years observing them.

How long a rookery will remain in a certain place I have never been able to ascertain, but an old countryman once told me that there had been one near his home at Sandhurst as long as he could remember, and he was 84 years of age at that time.

When a rookery is in existence, and the nests have not been entirely destroyed by the elements, the birds do not always make new nests each year, but will renovate the old ones either by taking twigs form the broken nests or using newly gathered material. There is much animation when building operations are taking place, and a great deal of noise is caused when the birds—with thieving habits typical of the crow family—take twigs from the nests of other birds.

Nests are made of twigs of various thicknesses and consolidated with mud; roots, grass and sometimes straw being used for lining Eggs, which may be form three to six are of a greenish colour mottled olive-brown.

The carrion crow is often confused with the rook, but if a close inspection is made of the two birds it will be seen that the adult rook has a bare whitish patch round the base of the bill, whereas the feathers of the crow extend right up to the base of the bill.

Carrion crows can generally be distinguished from rooks by their much slower and measured flight, keeping together in pairs.

and nesting in isolated trees.

As a result of much persecution the rooks have had to live more or less by their wits, but by becoming wise and wily have managed to flourish.

If anyone doubts their wisdom, try to approach them with anything that resembles a gun and see them lift into the air and sail away to a safe distance. Truly it can be said: "A wise bird is the rook."

*   *   *

ALL IN A DAY'S FISHING

A farmer invited me for a day's fishing in Gloucestershire, and a friend named Joe accompanied me on a very hot day.

As we walked along the bank of a stream a big fish rose to the surface, giving promise of a good day.

Joe, a very keen novice, wanted to get at this big fellow immediately, but I felt that it was necessary to pay a courtesy visit to the farmer before commencing to cast a fly; so, leaving him with this intention I suggested that he should not on any account cast over this fish as his tackle was not strong enough to take it.

On returning, I discovered that the eagerness of my companion had set aside my advice, and he had well and truly got into the big fish, which was held at that moment by something under water.

Lying in the stream on the opposite side was a withy tree that had been blown down, the direction of the line indicating that the cause of the hold up might be one of the branches; now arose the problem of how to get it.

The farmer arrived just at this time and suggested that the branches be cut off and, after fetching a saw he went away to a distant field to carry on with his day's task.

Joe kept his hold on the rod while I made an attempt to sever the branches by standing on one below water and holding with one hand the only branch above water. I discarded my coat, trousers, and socks, retaining my nailed shoes to get a grip on the slippery surface.

Some of these branches were fairly thick, and this became a tiring job with a saw that was not very sharp, added to the fact that the sawing had to be done under water. It took nearly an hour to sever four of the branches, and the fish had not yet moved.

The branch I was holding was a very flexible one, and thankful I was too, for the water was now above my knees, and it was necessary to get much deeper for the next cut. My tired arm had just forced the saw through another branch when, losing the grip on the one above, I dropped to the bottom of the stream, with water now up to the waist.

The cutting of the last limb released the line, but I think that in falling my feet landed on the fish and injured it, for it came to the surface in a dazed condition where Joe netted it.

Imagine, however, my surprise on turning my head to see the farmer's wife watching the proceedings! What a predicament! How could a half-naked man get out of the water in these circumstances?

Added to my dilemma was the fact that I was standing in soft mud and still going down. Nothing could have been more fortunate than the farmer reappearing on the scene, just as the water reached my beard.

He told me to "hang on" while he fetched a towel and some under-clothing, and, to my great relief his wife accompanied him! Return-ing soon with the towel, clothing, and rope, he and Joe helped me back to dry land again.

Needless to say it was with some embarrassment that I faced the farmer's wife when we sat down in the house to have some refresh-ment!

We didn't cast another fly that day, being very contented with a trout that weighed 5½lb.; one that secured us a bottle of whisky for a specimen fish.

Perhaps it was not captured in the approved manner, but it provided us with all the excitement we needed for one day.

*   *   *

IT'S A HARD LIFE FOR GAMEKEEPERS

The unions representing employees are continually asking for shorter working hours, but there is one man in the countryside who, by the nature of his occupation, has no time to think about regular hours.

This is the gamekeeper, ever on the alert day and night, partic-ulary during the summer when he is rearing pheasants and trying to keep them within bounds for the shooting parties in the winter time.

Much work has to be done in the spring to trap and shoot what he terms "vermin," for if this is not done stoats, weasels, hawks, magpies, carrion crows and foxes may cause him a lot of trouble later on.

I have enjoyed many days with a keeper and learned much about woodcraft and the haunts and habits of wild creatures.

As most of his time is occupied in the open air he gets familar with every sight and sound in the fields and woods around him.

He may not have a close acquaintance with scientific text-books regarding Nature, but he is well equiped with knowledge that has been gained by keen observation and practical experience.

When pheasants are reared on some estates today the eggs may be purchased from a game farm and then hatched in incubators, but when I used to accompany the gamekeeper we had to search for nests in the spring and collect the eggs.

Broody hens—or bantams—had to be purchased to do the necessary hatching.

The most anxious period for any gamekeeper is from the time the young birds (and hens) are taken in their coops to the rearing field and coverts until shooting takes place and the adult birds are safely in the bag.

There is much work to be done in the preparation of food for the young and feeding them; and every precaution has to be taken when they are running free from the coops, to guard against the many winged and four-footed predators that are ever on the watch.

Placing thick string—treated with a strong repellent—around the boundaries of the rearing field or coverts, or lighted lamps at night, may act as a partial deterrent, but even this does not always prevent losses.

From early morning when the young are released, until they are safely back in the coops and locked up late at night the keeper cannot relax his constant vigil.

He is helped considerably by the birds around him, for the chatter of a magpie, or the alarm note of a blackbird or wren indicates to him that there is an 'enemy' in the neighbourhood.

When birds can use their wings it is not easy to keep them within bounds, but with constant feeding on the keeper's territory it is hoped they will return to the place where they know food can be found.

The first day that shooting takes place is an important one for the gamekeeper, for it is then that he hopes to see the result of all his hard labour; the bigger the 'bag' the better he is pleased.

This will depend very largely on the quality of the shooting, and nothing displeases a keeper more than to see birds being put over the "guns" and allowed to get away.

On one occasion I stood by a titled gentleman who fired over 50 cartridges and only one pheasant came down—and that was a runner that got away! He turned to me and said: "I never could shoot."

Perhaps it was a good thing that he never heard what the keeper said.

*   *   *

ANGLER DIVED IN TO RETRIEVE HIS HOOK

Until I watched a man fishing at Wainlodes it had never occurred to me an angler could be concerned at the possible loss of a hook !

During the time I was sitting near him the hook on his line became entangled in the root of an overhanging tree, and, pulling hard to dislodge it he broke the line.

After putting on a bathing costume he then dived into the water and secured the hook. When he was on the bank again I said to him: "You went to a lot of trouble to get that hook." "I did," he replied, "that's the only hook I've got—and it cost me fourpence !"

He tied the hook on the line and put on bait then cast it into the water, and to my astonishment placed the rod on the bank and then dived into the water again to have a swim!

Most anglers keep their eyes on the movement of the float for a possible bite, but this didn't, and I have seen two others who thought it unnecessary. One was sitting in a boat-tied to a pier— with the bottom end of his rod fixed in a hole of an unused boat-seat, and at the top of the rod was a bell which rang if a fish tugged at the bait. While waiting for something 'to turn up' the angler smoked his pipe and read a newspaper!

Another man—with an original idea I thought—did not use a rod. He first took off one of his shoes and a sock, and then baited his hook before throwing it into the water.

After the line and bait sank to some considerable distance he put a loop in the spare end and attached it to his wrist, with the line resting between two toes!

Whether he caught anything in this unusual manner I did not wait to see, but when I left him he was lying peacefully on his back enjoying the morning sunshine.

In the 'Citizen' some years ago appeared the heading: "Fishing with a withy stick and bent pin."

A friend of mine, named Jim, after walking along the bank of the Severn one day, sat down to eat some sandwiches. Near him was a withy stick, and attached to it was a piece of string and bent pin; probably left there by a child.

To amuse himself he put a piece of bread on the pin and threw it into the water Shortly afterwards a man approached him and asked if he had a licence. Jim scoffed at the idea, but the man was not in the mood for jocularity.

He insisted of having Jim's name and address, and on this being given the visitor departed.

Jim was still laughing about the incident when he told me the following day, but a few days later the smile had disappeared from his face when he said that he had been summoned to appear before the magistrates for fishing without a licence.

Jim was a well-known figure and law-abiding citizen, and he felt that the magistrates would overlook this trivial offence, but, despite his plea of innocence he had to pay a fine of 5s. The payment of this was a minor detail, but the amount of publicity given to the case was a major calamity for poor Jim.

*   *   *

HE HOOKED TWO PIKE IN ONE

Looking back over many years, I often recall some of the curious things about the countryside that puzzled me at the time.

One of them occurred near Eastnor Castle while fishing from a boat for pike in the adjoining lake.

A small pike was hooked, but when pulling it in I was surprised to see another pike clinging tenaciously to the tail part of it!

I know that pike, when hungry, will eat each other, and often take creatures swimming on the water; on one occasion I saw a young duckling taken from the inside of a pike completely whole and not even crushed.

With a view to finding an answer to this question I consulted an expert angler. He told me: "The teeth on the palate of a pike are directed backwards towards the gullet, and can be depressed in order to facilitate the entrance of the prey, and as they cannot be pressed in the opposite direction they effectively prevent any chance of escape."

Something which puzzled me for many years was the drumming of woodpeckers; whether the sounds of it was produced solely by the beak making contact with the tree, or by some other means.

When I asked a naturalist he wrote: "When a woodpecker produces drumming sounds with its beak, these sounds are amplified by the deliberate use of the resonance cavity in the birds head.

"The bird not only has muscular power and strong head for the job, but there are hollows in the bones and spaces in its beak and mouth which combine to produce a surge of sound-waves roaring out in sympathy with the oscillations reaching them.

"Controlled breathing and the disposition of the bird's tongue also play their parts in perfecting the amplifications of what's best described as a percussion sound."

I told him of my striking rapidly on a tree with the handle of a pocket-knife where a woodpecker had been drumming, and the sound of this could not be heard by a friend standing 200 yards away, and of this he wrote: "You can't hope to compete with a bird which has perfected a fairly complex musical instrument."

77

Many people saw on television the excellent film of woodpeckers made by Heinz Sielmann, and may have read his book "My year with the woodpeckers." In this he wrote of the reason for the drumming: "The loud hammer blows of the woodpeckers beak are signals whereby he can communicate with other woodpeckers up to threequarters of a mile away," and, "each woodpecker recognises the drumming rhythm of its own particular species."

Another problem just before Christmas a farmer gave me permission to cut some mistletoe from apple trees in an orchard containing in-calf cows, and said: "Don't drop any of the berries on the ground." When asking the reason for this he said: "If they cows eat any of them berries they be liable to 'slip' (abort) their calves."
Can this be true?

*   *   *

A CHAPEL DEACON'S ENCOUNTER WITH THE POLICE CHIEF

Many years ago, town tradesmen used a pony and cart when delivering goods to country customers. One very well-known grocer, making his last call at a house in a Gloucestershire village was asked by a man who occupied it if he would like to buy a brace of pheasants for five shillings, game then being out of season. He purchased the birds, then tossed them into the back of the cart and proceeded towards home.

Soon after he started the journey, another horse-driven conveyance passed him, travelling in the same direction.

"Good afternoon, Mr. Smith," shouted the passenger.

On turning his head, the grocer had a shock when he saw that the man who greeted him was a superintendant of police. A few seconds earlier, thought Mr. Smith, he might have been caught "in possession of game." A lucky escape. . .

Conscience was his biggest enemy and, as the horse jogged along, poor Smith imagined all sorts of things that could happen to him in the way of punishment. He could, if the magistrates were considerate, be let off with a fine, but they might send him to gaol. . .

He had travelled nearly a mile when he noticed that the police conveyance had pulled up by the side of the road, and he received a signal to stop. "Now I'm for it," thought Smith.

"My vehicle has broken down," said the superintendent and I have an urgent appointment. Can you oblige me with a lift?"

The Super's foot was already on the step of the cart, and well — what could he do? He didn't want to refuse, neither did he want the "evidence" to be seen. He could be charged with poaching, and he — a deacon of the Chapel!

They both occupied the same seat and, fortunately (thought the frightened grocer) were both facing the same direction towards home.

So that the passenger might not get an opportunity to turn round to see the birds in the back of the cart. Smith did his best to engage him in conversation.

It was a great relief to him when his passenger alighted at police headquarters. He was thanked by the Super and, as an after thought it seemed, he was told that there were some very nice pheasants in the cart. Poor Smith nearly collapsed. Trembling with fear, he managed to splutter out: "Yes would you like one?" The offer was readily accepted and the recipient hurried away to keep his appointment.

The story should end here–but on Monday Smith answered a knock on his door, and he received a shock when he saw that the caller was a police sergeant.

"The Superintendent would like to see you at the police station at once," he said.

Smith's spirits sank to zero. He thought immediately of the pheasants, and imagine himself before the court.

He made his way to the station and knocked timidly on the door marked "Superintendent."

A voice resembling a clap of thunder invited him to come in.

How he entered he never knew, but he had a faint recollection of going in and standing on a mat in front of the Super.

"Good morning," came from a voice behind a big black moustache–not the voice he had heard when being thanked for a lift.

"On the 12th of July you were found in possession of pheasants during the close season. Do you agree?"

"Yes replied the trembling grocer, "you had one.'

"I took that as evidence against you," said the Super.

For five minutes the nerve–racked grocer was subjected to such a lecture that he was on the point of collapse. Then a sergeant was called and told to fetch a parcel from an adjoining room. This was brought and given to Smith with these words: "It has always been my contention that game always tastes better when you you have fish to go with it."

In the parcel was the best cut from a 20 lb. salmon which the police had taken from a poacher on the Severn the previous night.

Who shall say that the police are not human?

*   *   *

79

THE WHIMSICAL PEOPLE OF YUBBERTON

The small village of Yubberton is situated in a very remote part of the county, and the inhabitants there at the beginning of this century were much as you would expect in a spot so secluded.

When I was there I heard some of their sayings and became acquainted with their customs. Anything and everything which had to do with a death or funeral had a special fascination for them.

When 'old man' Sparrow passed away a friend of his named Joe called at his home to offer his condolences to the son who was arranging the burial.

Joe asked to see the deceased and when shown into the room where the old man lay he said: "'E looks well, don't 'e?," and the son agreed with him, but suggested that the reason he looked so well was that his father had recently returned from a fortnight's holiday at the seaside !

Unknown to Jim or the son an unusual thing happened in the preparation of the grave. The sexton started to dig the grave one day, but when darkness came he left it, to be completed the next day.

Later that night a man, who had stayed too long at the inn, was walking through the churchyard to get to his home when he fell into the half-dug grave, and promptly went to sleep.

The following morning the sexton to his surprise, found the man lying there, but was not greatly astonished when he saw who it was. He woke him, and the man without word got up at once and then looking round the churchyard, said: "I reckon I be about the first chap up this resurrection mornin'."

There was always great anxiety among the people if a person was in a critical condition, and the number that crowded round the bedside sometimes caused embarrassment, but on one occasion there was a Job's comforter among them who told an ailing man with the kindest intention, not to cherish false hopes. "Ah, George" he said, "it isn't they that feels the most that dies the most."

In writing this I remember so many priceless sayings, and one in particular was that of a woman, with a world of sympathy in her voice, of the ailing girl who was sitting in the room of her cottage: "as I tell her, poor girl, it will be a merciful day when we hear the bells a' tolling for her."

Many of us keep and cherish articles that remind us of some special event, or, perhaps have given us some pleasure during our life, but it was a surprise to hear of one woman who treasured a pewter teapot because, to use her own words: "It has seen more funerals than any other in the village — seventeen, all told."

Not only had it done duty for the family, but when other inhabitants of the village had passed away.

The squire of the village who was known as 'the queer chap at

Gloucester Carnival The pig would not join in the chorus

the Manor' had a thatched roof placed over a trout stream to keep the fish dry, and created much bad feeling when he dismissed a local girl form his services.

He admitted to the mother of the girl that she was an excellent servant, but he could not overlook the one fault she possessed. "She's flighty ! he said. "She would leave the house three times for every once she came in."

*   *   *

GETTING TO KNOW PEOPLE IN THE COUNTRY

For over 40 years my work enabled me to travel a very wide area, extending over large parts of Gloucestershire, Worcestershire and Wiltshire.

I had many opportunities to gain some knowledge of this subject.

Interviewing country people of every description daily also gave me an insight into human nature.

What was my work ? Even the chief of my department was in doubt ! When I entered his room one day he said to another member of the staff : "Ah ! here is a man who has the best job in the department. He comes into the office in the morning, has a look through the window, and if it is a fine day he decides that it is a good day to visit the Cotswolds. Nobody knows where he goes; and nobody knows what he does."

It was not, however, always fine on the Cotswolds when I had to make a journey there, for I have vivid memories of the terrible conditions which existed in the winters of 1939 and 1947, when the countryside was buried in snow and ice.

Birds were frozen to the branches of the trees on which they perched, and four-footed animals died because they could not get food; one rabbit I saw climbed up the frozen snow to eat the bark of a tree, 10 feet from the ground.

Telegraph poles carrying heavy wires lay on the ground, and one piece which I took home, about 15 inches in length, weighed 3½ lbs.

A strange thing was that the weight of ice on wires caused two routes of poles to collapse—from the bottom to the top of Cleeve Hill—yet from the top of the Hill to Winchcombe not a pole was out of place, and only two wires broken.

Some of the wires, over-hanging a country garden, caused damage to a woman's clothes hanging on a line on washing day. Damages were claimed, and when I called on the claiment some time later I asked if I could see the damaged garments. "No, you can't" said the woman, "I've got them on !"

82

Incidentally, one condition of my employment was that when interviewing members of the public I should use tact, i.e. 'nice perception in seeing and doing exactly what is best in the circumstances".

In these days the cost of labour is very high, but several years ago a farmer told me at Dymock that he could obtain the services of one labourer at any time without having to pay him wages.

All he had to do was to provide the man with plenty of cider and a 'bit of bread and cheese', and to do the work the labourer walked to and from Newent each day.

Farmers use all kinds of methods in an endeavour to prevent crows and other birds from destroying growing crops, but one unusual scarecrow I saw in a field at Coaly was a brown stuffed bear, erected so that it sat on its haunches.

On many occasions I have seen sheep lying on their backs in fields and unable to get on their feet; these I have turned over. But one incident almost got me into trouble.

I walked across a field to look at a cow lying down; it was dead and I informed the owner who lived nearby. Some weeks later I met him, and he informed me that the cow had died as a result of anthrax, which is communicable to human beings a danger I did not foresee.

Feeling greatly relieved I invited the farmer to have a drink at the local inn. He said he would have beer, but when I called for a gin and Italian vermouth he said he would like to have the same.

The landlord produced two bottles and tumbler glasses and told us to help ourselves which we did. The price ? Six pence for each glass.

*   *   *

PLEASURE TO SEE A JAY EMERGING FROM A WOOD

In such an extensive area as the Forest of Dean, with trees of many varieties, one would expect to find many kinds of birds, but in my long association with this locality I found that though they were plentiful in some parts, in others they are conspicuous by their absence..

The place birds choose are generally those which have a variety of trees with plenty of bushes for undergrowth and, perhaps most important, where they can obtain food.

On several occasions I have walked miles through the Forest, where the only trees were of oak with no undergrowth, and have not seen a bird of any description. Yet where there is a mixture of trees many can be seen.

One of the most prominent of birds to 'catch the eye' is the jay, a bird that has been persecuted for ages by man; even now advertisements appear of buyers requiring their feathers for making the flies needed by anglers for catching salmon and trout.

It is one of the pleasures for me to see a jay emerging from a wood, and perhaps catch a momentary vision of a white rump as it disappears with that familiar undulating flight.

It is undoubtedly more wary and shy than many other birds, but when I have been in a 'hide' there have been many opportunities to observe it at close quarters, and what a glorious creature it is !

Surely this is one of the most handsome of the crow family, with the rich chestnut plumage of its body, the dainty crest on the head incessantly rising and falling, and wing-coverts with their alternating bars of blue, black and white; one of the most pleasing ornaments of our woods.

A friend of mine who was employed by the Forestry Commissioners—a keen observer of bird-life—used to inform me when he had found the nest of a bird that he thought would be of interest to me.

At the first opportunity I would meet and accompany him to the site, and perhaps it would be the nest of a goldcrest.

The frail-looking structure is generally made on the underside of a branch, with materials consisting of moss, wool, spider's webs, lichens and others of a similar nature, while feathers are used for the lining.

When entering a wood one of the first sounds to be heard may be tap-tap-tap or the 'laugh' of a woodpecker, and the sight of the larger variety, the green woodpecker, with its beautiful colouring of olive green on the back shading into yellow, with crimson crown and nape, is something to admire.

It needs a sharp eye to detect the quiet colours of tree-creepers on the trunks of some trees with which these harmonise so well but I have been fascinated watching them in the Forest as they move upwards, downwards, and round the trunk of a tree hunting for insects in the crevices of the bark.

Other birds, clinging to the bark of a tree with movements somewhat similar to the tree-creepers, are the nut-hatches, and what is remarkable about these birds is the quantity of material they use when making a nest.

If they find a hole in a tree too big for their use they will reduce it to their own size by the skilful use of clay, and it has been recorded that one nest made in a haystack contained 11 pounds of clay, while another, in a nest-box, comprised about three pounds of clay and over 1,000 pieces of silver birch-bark.

* * *

QUARTET OF COUNTRY WOMEN

Many articles I have written about the countryside concerned men who lived there, but now I would like to relate a few incidents about four different kinds of country women living in Gloucestershire villages which I often visited.

One of my early visits was to interview an owner of a house that stood in grounds surrounded by a high wall. There was a small door in the wall through which I entered, and then a paved footway a few yards in length to the door of the house.

After I rang the bell a maid answered it, and when I told her the nature of my call and asked to see the owner she went indoors to inform her mistress. And, judging by the noise in the house she found her !

A hefty woman with a very red face and bulging eyes appeared and in a voice that one associates with a disgruntled army sergeant major she yelled: "What's the idea of coming to the back door of a house to see a lady? Don't you realise that the correct thing to do is to go to the front door ?"

Without listening to the reason for my call she hurriedly departed, and as I walked my mind turned to thoughts of human weaknesses that are common in many of us.

When looking at a newspaper some weeks later I read that nearly two tons of lead had been stolen from the roof of her house when she was on holiday and, though it may seem an unkind thought, I could not feel sorry for her.

When I was driving a car along a main road once a small dog ran into the road from the gateway, and it appeared so suddenly that I had no chance of pulling up to avoid striking the animal.

When I did stop and go back to see if the dog was injured a woman appeared, and before I had an opportunity to explain to her what had happened she shouted, "You'd better get your cheque book out."

Fortunately the dog was not badly injured, but it seemed a strange thing that this woman should be more concerned with getting money than being anxious about the welfare of the dog, or the cause of the accident.

What a pleasure it was to interview another woman, who could rightly be called a lady, when I saw her at her lonely home in the Cotswolds; she was an elderly widow who lived alone.

There was deep snow on the ground when I knocked on her door, and on being invitied into her rooms she was full of apologies because there was no fire there.

I saw an electric fire in the room, and she explained to me that her son had sent it to her two years before, but she didn't know how to use it. Electricity was installed in the house, and cable and socket were in the room; it never occurred to her to 'plug in' and switch on the heat !

My knowledge of electricity is practically nil, but I was most anxious to help her if possible. I could find nothing to indicate the voltage or current on the electric fire, and was unable to ascertain from the switch-board in the kitchen whether the system was alternating or direct current.

Should I take the risk and 'plug in' the fire ? Anxious to bring a bit of warmth into the home of this charming old lady I switched off the current at the switch-board, and then put the plug of the fire into the socket.

I asked her to watch the fire while I switched on the current, and a few moments later she walked into the kitchen with the most radiant smile that I have ever seen and said; "Oh! sir it works ! !"

It was a great comfort to me that the chance I had taken did not end in disaster !

There were many tragedies in the 1914-1918 war, when parents lost their sons, girls lost their sweethearts and wives lost their husbands; the story of one woman whose husband 'reported missing' was a particularly sad one.

She lived in a Gloucester village about two miles from the nearest railway station and for years I travelled to and from this station.

On several occasions I saw a woman, either on the platform or walking to and from the station, but never in the company of another person.

During a conversation with the stationmaster he told me the cause of the frequent visits by this woman. So confident was she that her missing husband would return that she wanted to be at the station to meet him again, and she never gave up hope until her death many years later.

*   *   *

WELCOME. "Pretty late home, weren't you ? Was the wife annoyed?" "Was she annoyed ? I'll say she was! She left a note - "Slippers in the refrigerator."

GET WELL SOON. "I want some grapes for my sick husband. Do you know if any poison has been sprayed on these ?" "No, mum; you'll have to get that at the chemists."

NEEDY. Tearaway; "Excuse me, sir, but could you spare a little something for a poor fellow who has nothing in the world but a sawn off shot gun ?"

STICKING IT OUT. "Has your husband got another job yet, Mrs. Murphy?" asked her neighbour. "Sure, and he has, Mrs. O'Hara. It's hard work , and it's killing him - but thanks be, it's permanent."

HOW ONE OLD MAN TOLD THE WEATHER

At one time it was my belief that the older countrymen were very good forecasters of the weather, but I did not know if they did it by their own astronomical observations or had a sense which townsmen did not possess.

The answer to my question on the subject, put to an old-timer on the Cotswolds, was very different from what I expected.

I wanted to find out the name of the owner of a field, and for this purpose walked across it to find out from a farm worker who was then ploughing the land.

During our conversation he released the horses from the plough, and then told me that he was going to take the animals back to their stables.

As the work was not completed I asked him why he was "knocking off" so early.

"'Cause it be goin' to rain," he said. At the time the sky was beautifully clear with not a cloud in sight so, being curious as usual I asked him how he knew.

He replied: "I sid it in Old Moore's Almanac afore I cum out this mornin'."

Later that day I visited a farmer for permission to place some telegraph poles on his property, and it was necessary to convey him in my van to his property about a mile away.

On the journey he glanced into the back of the van and said: "Don't you carry any tools?"

I answered in the negative "What's the idea of giving you a van if you don't carry anything in it?"

I explained to him that I had to visit many farmers, and if one had a sack of potatoes, a four-and-half barrel of cider, or a pot of apples to give away there was plenty of room in the van to take them.

He laughed loudly, then said: "Do you ever get over-loaded?"

During my journeys around the countryside I have had many requests for a lift, particularly in the war period.

Perhaps the most embarassing one was being asked by a woman living in a lonely cottage on the Cotswolds to take her to Cirencester hospital as she was expecting a "happy event" at any moment; needless to say it was a great relief to me when arriving at the destination.

She was full of gratitude; very different from a man I encountered on the road near Tetbury.

There is a couplet about this town which says: "Two totally tired, toads tried to trot to Tetbury," and it was just at the time I was trying to twist my tongue around this that I saw a man with a carpenter's bag on his shoulder trotting towards Tetbury.

He stopped me and asked: "How much farther is it to Kemble Station, guv'nor ?" I told him he was going in the wrong direction; he had in fact, walked two miles in the wrong direction.

He said he was going to a job in Swindon, and must catch the 12 o'clock train; it was then 11.30.

As he appeared to be a genuine workman and anxious to get the job offered him, I turned the vehicle around and said I would take him to the station which was three miles away.

On arrival he not only forgot to say "thank you," but had the audacity to ask me if I would pay his fare to Swindon!

On the return journey it was necessary to pull up because all the water had gone from the radiator, and here I was stuck on the road miles from habitation. At the bottom of a bank about 50 yards away was a pond, covered in ice. After much searching on a rubbish tip I found a small sauce bottle, and it must have taken well over a hundred journeys to get sufficient water to be able to start the engine again.

What I thought of the "genuine workman" can be left to the imagination!

Perhaps the most unwelcome "passengers" I had to contend with occurred on a very hot day, when it was necessary to open the windscreen to get some fresh air, for I ran into hundreds of bees and must have collected the whole swarm!

*   *   *

GOING SHOOTING?
MAKE SURE OF YOUR RIGHTS FIRST

When making arrangements with an owner of property to rent the shooting for the season, it is better if the terms, and the definition of the boundaries, are stated in a written agreement.

In two instances a partner and myself failed to do this, resulting in what the owners of the land called "a misunderstanding."

After paying the owner of some property his fee, we set out for a day's shooting, but on arriving at the site were astonished to see three men with guns and dog walking across a ploughed field, the dog in search of rabbits and the men preparing to shoot any that got up.

They expressed surprise at seeing us with guns, and we did likewise. They said they had bought the rights to shoot there, and what were we doing on the land ?

Naturally, it lead to some argument when we explained that we, too, had paid for the right to be there.

When we met the owner some time later he said that the other party had only the right 'to catch rabbits with the use of nets and ferrets,' yet they had openly ignored this.

This was a most unsatisfactory arrangement, for not only had the owner taken shooting rights fees from two parties but, in addition and without our knowledge, he also employed an ex-game-keeper to catch rabbits for him, and these he sold in the market.

Obtaining revenue from three sources might have given great satisfaction to the owner of the land, but for us it was a sheer waste of money.

Another thing that we did not anticipate was that on three sides of some of this property was land owned by a man who reared and shot game-birds, and he owned the hedges and ditches which divided the land; the ditches being on 'our' side of the hedges.

His gamekeeper would get over a fence and walk regularly along 'our' side of the ditches, and with the aid of his dog drive out any birds that might be in the hedges.

Whether he had a legal right to do this might be questionable; even if he had, his continual presence on our domain did much to spoil our day's sport.

The next incident concerns boundaries on another 'shoot' we rented, and here my partner experienced some trouble through a misunderstanding.

There was a wood (unfenced) on this land, and we were told by the owner of the land that the whole of this wood was included in the letting.

On our first appearance the ferrets were put into a 'bury' near a dry ditch approximately in the centre of the wood.

After firing a few shoots a man appeared and accused us of poaching on his land and said he would prosecute us. He asked for our names and addresses, which we gave him, and then went away in an angry mood.

This unfenced ditch extended from end to end of the wood, and, unknown to us, it divided two separate pieces of land. Subsequently we saw the owner who was paid for the shooting and explained what had happened, and he admitted that he failed to tell us of this dividing line.

As we were undoubtedly on the wrong side of it, and anxious to avoid prosecution, the rightful owner was then approached and an apology made to him.

After a lengthy discussion he agreed to forego proceedings if we agreed to make a contribution to a hospital — which we were pleased to do ?

Although these incidents happened many years ago such things do not quickly fade from the memory.

THIRTY YEARS AN EXILE—BUT HIS VOICE HAD THE MARK OF HIS ORIGIN

Born in a Gloucestershire village, where my roots are, I have always seized every opportunity to learn something about the countryside, and now that I am of what is termed 'advanced age' the memories of what I have experienced is something which is treasured.

Perhaps it is the smell of new-mown hay or a field of beans in flower; watching a craftsman building a Cotswold wall; the thatching of a roof, or rick of corn; a stoat and its method of catching a rabbit; kestrels swooping to the ground to pick up a mouse; the flighting of birds and their nesting habits; a hedgehog rolling into a ball when alarmed; the furtive look in the eye of a fox; and the many other things, all of which can be enjoyed by those who have eyes to see and ears to hear.

Apart from living in Gloucestershire most of my life, I have had the pleasure of living in and seeing much of the countryside in Somerset, Devon and Cornwall.

The character of the countryman in these counties does not vary considerably, but their dialects do, and even if they move from their particular county to another one they do not, generally, lose their own dialect.

One instance of this was when I met a man, about 50 years of age, who had recently taken a farm near Dymock. Immediately he spoke I was able to tell him the county from which he came.

In a rich Devon voice he said: "I don't know how you guessed that, for I've been farming in Yorkshire for the past 30 years."

Despite living for this period in a county where the dialect is very broad he had never lost his own, and this is only one of the many cases I have encountered.

With all the good gifts that have been bestowed on us by nature—and all free—I have been amazed to meet so many people in the past who have visited the countryside and found nothing of interest; they have even called it a dull place !

There were not a great many people taking an interest in natural history when I was a youth, and anything I learned was by having an inquisitive mind.

Without the aid of a tutor, or access to books, the only method I could adopt was a practical one; "Seek and ye shall find."

Now, due to the excellent natural history talks that have been given on television and radio, many more people have been enlightened on the subject and are anxious to make themselves familiar with it.

Incidentally, I don't think that several people going out together to study wild-life—except those accompanied by a guide and hidden in a bird sanctuary—will learn much about it.

Every bird and animal looks upon a human being as a potential danger, and the slightest movements or noise created by a would-be observer will cause it to depart in haste.

The most successful way to do it is alone, and can only be done by tremendous patience.

For attracting some of the four-footed animals my method is to hide in a wood and imitate the 'squeal' of a rabbit, but, to be effective, this requires a long experience and much practice.

*   *   *

COTSWOLD JOURNEY REVIVES MEMORIES

It is sometimes said that anyone returning to the district of his origin discovers that people and places are not quite the same as before, but in a trip I made recently the countryside has not changed very much, and it is just as beautiful as before.

Improved methods of agriculture have been made, of course, and this was the most noticeable feature of my journey.

In the 'old days' it was not unusual to see fields of corn containing large quantities of poppies and thistles, but on this occasion I did not see a field with any of these weeds; wheat, barley and oats were all upstanding and looking clean and in first class condition.

As a boy, on my grand-father's farm, I used to tie up the sheaves of corn, which had been cut with a scythe, and I can well remember the number of thistles that made my task a very uncomfortable and painful one.

The district travelled included Painswick Beacon, Cranham Village, Miserden, Beech Pike, Elkstone, Colesborne, Withington, Stowell Park, Chedworth, then back to Gloucester via Fossebridge, Compton Abdale, Kilkenny, Seven Springs, and Crickley Hill.

This is a journey I can recommend to anyone — little traffic will be encountered — and there will be many opportunities of seeing some of the best scenery in the county.

As I was a passenger in the car my eyes were free to take in all my surroundings, and many places reminded me of incidents that happened years ago when I travelled the district.

At Painswick Beacon I thought of an unusual incident that happened when I once played golf there. On what was then the sixth hole it was necessary to play the first stroke over a hill to a green that was not visible. After climbing up the hill to the green, I could see no sight of the ball. An old man standing near the green, said: "Are you looking for your ball?"

I assured him that I was, but I could not find it. When, eventually,

91

I arrived at the club house and told another member of this incident he said that the crafty old man was in the habit of waiting at 'blind' holes for a ball, standing on it and pressing into the ground with his foot, and later offering it for sale to anyone willing to buy it !

Visiting one village was a reminder of a curious legal document shewn to me by an old mole catcher.

It was an agreement, duly stamped, between landlords and tenants on the one part, and Rogers and Sons, mole catchers, of the same parish, on the other part, the latter undertaking "to kill and destroy the moles, on or in all such lands as the said owners respectively hold in the parish, for the sum of twopence per acre the first year, and for the sum of one penny per acre annually for and during a term of 14 years next ensuring from the date hereof."

The owners of the said lands on their part undertaking to pay the sum agreed on — "the moles being caught efficiently" — a very important proviso. No date was on the agreement, but I can only assume it was in 'the good old days.'

When in Stowell Park some years ago I was unfortunate enough to see scores of rabbits suffering from myxomatosis — something I never wish to see again — but this time I only saw one rabbit, apparently free from this terrible disease.

The great charm of the whole area I visited is the feeling of peace which pervades the scene. In some of the villages a few houses have been built in recent years, but I was pleased to find that the builders had given much thought to them so that they blended well with the surroundings.

The churches, the unspoilt villages, the wonderful scenery, and the general appearance of the countryside made this a journey that will long remain in my memory.

*   *   *

REJECTION ORIENTAL. A would-be international writer received the following from a Chinese firm of publishers. "We read your manuscript with boundless delight. By the sacred ashes of our ancestors, we swear that we have never dipped into a book of such overwhelming mastery. If we were to publish this book, it would be impossible in the future to issue any other book of a lower standard. As this is unlikely in the next ten thousand years, we are to our regret compelled to return it to you, and beg a thousand times that you will forgive our action."

RABBIT TURNED THE TABLES ON THE STOAT—

PROTECTING YOUNG?

Many people have seen a stoat in pursuit of a rabbit, and noted how incapable of resistance the latter appears to be, but on occasions I have seen the tables turned by rabbits chasing stoats.

Unfortunately I have never seen what happened at the end of the chase as the animals either ran into a wood or disappeared through a hedge.

In each case when the rabbit pursued the stoat it could, perhaps, be assumed that it was a doe defending her young.

Nature has given stoats and other animals some power to overcome their prey and so obtain food; but are the victims, in fact, paralysed, or is it just curiosity that keeps them watching for instance, a stoat rolling and stumbling before their eyes?

When sitting near a wood at Bibury it amazed me to see a small weasel — an animal which generally preys on small animals like rodents — "shadowing" a large hare without the latter making any attempt to escape.

When one thinks of the long legs of the hare—probably the fastest runner of any of our animals—it was strange to watch it just sit and await its fate.

Why it did not make use of its tremendous speed to get away is yet another of Nature's mysteries.

Many animals can swim if necessary, but a rabbit doing so with a ferret on its back can be described as something unusal. While watching a gamekeeper ferreting on the sloping bank of the River Chelt at Boddington I saw a rabbit jump out of a burrow into the water and swim to the other side with the ferret hanging on to the back of its neck.

But this is not comparable with the feat of a domestic animal a one-day-old calf—swimming through half a mile of water with its mother and landing safely on the other side. The mother was scared into the water by dogs, and this remarkable occurrence was witnessed by three men.

Wild rabbits have been known to breed with tame, and there are many instances recorded, but my own knowledge of this is of them mixing together, with no definite evidence of the actual breeding.

During the last war I had to visit a remote part of the Cotswolds near Chedworth, and while in a small hut manned by two men of the RAF saw a tame doe rabbit waddle out from under a camp bed.

I ascertained from the men that they had a buck and doe which associated with the wild ones in the neighbourhood.

The buck was out at the time—had been for four days—and the doe would be absent occasionally, but they always returned.

Underneath the bed was a litter of week-old youngsters but whether they were the result of inter-breeding is not certain.

To try to find out I took one of the litter home, and with the aid of a fountain-pen filler and milk reared it in the house, eventually getting it on to solid food. It became very tame, but as the parents were similar in colour to the wild variety there was still no proof that it was the result of inter-breeding.

On my way home I pulled up near the boundary wall of a field in a narrow lane to have my lunch, and while reading the daily newspaper it suddenly became dark as an object hurtled through the air over the bonnet of the car.

Getting out to try to ascertain what it was I found that what appeared to be an apparition causing the 'black out' was a deer being pursued by a pack of fox-hounds!!

*   *   *

THE 'OLD ANCIENTS' SWAP TALES OF THE COUNTRY

Some time has elapsed since I last met those old countrymen Tom, Harry and Sam, so when I heard that they were meeting one evening at "The Old Tippling Philosopher" to celebrate Harry's eighty-fifth birthday it gave me an opportunity to join them again.

The landlord had such a great regard for this elderly trio — particularly Harry — that he provided all the refreshments free for this occasion.

When I arrived it was evident that the liquid refreshment had loosened their tongues and put them in a merry mood.

All the men were born on the Cotswolds, and like most elderly people they talked about the days of long ago. During the time I was there a note was made of a few of the stories.

Harry was comparing conditions of present day farm workers with those of his father and himself. "My father," he said, "used to get twelve shillings a week, and if 'e didn't go to church on Good Fridays 'e lost a day's wages, and 'told me that when I was born 'e buried 'is pipe in the garden 'cause 'e couldn't afford no tabacco.

"When I got married the wages was sixteen shillings a week, and my wife used to scrub the school to get a few bob extra.

"In the winter there was so much ice on the road 'er sometimes 'ad to crawl on her 'ands and knees to get there."

"We don't want to 'ear about them bad old days," said Tom. "What was that story you told me, Sam, when you was a game-keeper?"

"We was 'aving a shoot one day, said Sam," and after 'twas

over I was goin' round a wood to see if I could pick up any wounded birds. I 'appened to drop on Old Jim kneeling down by a 'edge and searching under a pile of bracken; 'e didn't see me coming.

Suddenly 'e pulled out a cock pheasant, one that 'ad just bin shot. When 'e looked up and saw me 'e grinned.

"'I've caught you this time, I said "Twas lyin' there when I comed past,' 'e said. I seed 'un and sez to myself, 'What a darned shame to leave that pheasant for some owd poacher chap to find.' Thinks I'd better tak' it to the keeper and be dammed if you didn't come along just as I was a goin' to tak'n up to your 'ouse."

"Was your father a game-keeper?" asked Tom. "Yes," said Sam, "'e was the man who discovered the Roman Villa at Chedworth when 'e was looking for a ferrer 'e 'ad lost."

"Tom, do you remember that night when we went catching sparrows round the vicarage ?" asked Sam, "Not 'alf I don't," replied Tom. "'Twas about the middle of the night when I'd got me net spread over the ivy on the wall near an open window, and you was shinin' your lamp into the net.

"Just as I was rubbin' the poles of me net up and down a servant in 'er nightdress and 'olding a lighted candle poked 'er 'ead out of the window right into me bloomin' net!"

When 'er saw us down below 'er screamed out and yelled for the police. I shut, me net up quick and we took to our 'eels, and when I got 'ome I found eight spodgers, the servant's night-cap and the candlestick stuck in me net!"

Harry had been sitting contently smoking his pipe and then said he wanted us to listen to a couple of his stories.

In early April a bishop was having a holiday on the Cotswolds, and when taking a walk across some fields he found Harry in charge of a flock of sheep.

"Good morning," he said, "What a large flock you have. How many sheep do you think you have there?"

"About 250 sir," replied Harry.

"I have a large flock, too," said the Bishop. "You don't look much like a shepherd to me sir! 'Ow many 'ave you got in your flock?" asked Harry.

"Well mine is a flock of a very different kind," came the reply, "it would probably amount to nearly ten thousand.

"Ten thousand!" said the startled Harry. "What sort of a lambin' season 'ave you 'ad?"

Harry took a good swig of his cider, and then continued; "Jim 'Arris and 'is brother Joe was shepherds, and they lived together in a cottage on a moor. Jim died, and the district nurse walked four miles across the moor to lay'n out.

"When 'er arrived Joe told 'er to go upstairs while 'e made a cup of tea for 'er.

95

"Just as 'er reached the stairs 'e said, "Dont 'e go to too much trouble wi'un, mind 'e were never a one ver tittivatin' isself."

*   *   *

THE CITY MAN WHO HAD NEVER SEEN

CRANHAM WOODS

During a conversation with a very active man in Gloucester, I told him of the natural beauty to be found everywhere within a few miles, and suggested that a ramble in the clean air would allow him to escape form the noise and congestion of the city.

He surprised me when he said that he had never seen Cranham Woods, or the trees at all seasons of the year, or the flowers that grow in the woods, fields, and near streams, and when I explained the beautiful scenery to be enjoyed from Painswick Beacon he was not at all impressed.

Well, we have the right to our likes and dislikes, but I wondered if there were others in the City who were unaware of the treasures they possessed in the surrounding countryside.

Perhaps I have had more opportunities than most people to see the countryside—for which I am thankful—and during my travels around Gloucestershire never a day passed without experiencing something new and interesting even on the Cotswolds in the very bad winters of 1939 and 1947.

Having very simple tastes I have enjoyed: the undulating nature of the Cotswolds with its woodlands and trout streams; the tithe barns and houses that blend so well with the countryside; leaves bursting forth in the spring and the glorious tints of autumn leaves; fruit trees in blossom; wild flowers; the smell of new-mown hay and beans in flower; shoeing of horses; cows being milked; and freshly-turned earth during ploughing.

Seeing a craftsman build a stone wall, or laying a hedge, and thatching; listening to the songs of birds at dawn; watching them flight and observing them making their nests and feeding the young;

Indulging in conversation with the genuine countryman, and listening to him speaking a language which is so easy to understand.

The history and records of old churches in the villages and hamlets are well worth investigation, and although many villages have become urbanised there are still several on the Cotswolds untouched by man that retain their old world charm and beauty, and where one gets a feeling that nothing much has happened since the dawn of creation.

The countryside is full of surprises, and by avoiding the main roads and making fullest use of the lanes and byways greater opportunities are afforded to make observations of Nature, and fill the mind with such delight that it will ever remain in the memory.

*   *   *

INCIDENTS IN THE GLO'SHIRE COUNTRYSIDE

As I travelled the old familar ground around the countryside of Gloucestershire recently, certain places revived memories of little episodes that occurred there.

First, near the "Royal William" at Cranham.

A well-known Gloucester dentist and myself attended a dinner there one evening, and when the party broke up it was found that 18 people were with no transport available to take them to their homes in Gloucester.

This dentist owned one of the very early model Ford cars—then often referred to as a Tin Lizzie—and in two journeys 20 passengers, including ourselves, were safely carried to their destination.

Some were squeezed inside the car, but the majority rode on the outside, clinging to the vehicle like limpets.

I shudder to think what might have happened if the brakes had failed to act descending the very steep Portway Hill.

Visiting Newent reminded me that when a gang of men worked on a development scheme there it became necessary to rent a building in which to lock up their stores.

This was obtained from a local farmer by the foreman and when the latter said "Where's the cider barrel, guv'nor?" he was told where the key of the shed could be found. The farmer never anticipated that his kind gesture would be abused. But it was.

In the two months that the gang worked (and wasted time) in the neighbourhood, the men consumed on the premises a tremendous quantity of the cider, and this, plus that taken home at night in bottles by each man, amounted to as much as two hogsheads; nearly 100 gallons. Such is gratitude.

Pulling up one day near the entrance gate of a farm on the Dymock road to eat my lunch, I saw a man nearby trimming a hedge with a long-handled hook.

Within a few moments a loud explosion was heard, and the man was seen to be holding his hands tightly to his face. As quickly as possible I hurried to his aid, finding him bleeding profusely from splintered glass.

Without more ado I put him in my car and rushed him to the farm, where it was possible to telephone and get immediate medical assistance.

The explosion was caused when the hook made contact with a bottle in the hedge. It contained a kind of liquid, but it was not possible to ascertain what it was as the bottle had been reduced to very small fragments.

I recalled meeting an old retired farmer in this district many years ago and visiting him several times. He was an extraordinary character.

Whenever I called to see him he would put his hand in his pocket and pull out a handful of sovereigns and half-sovereigns and say: "I'll give you some of these one day my boy." Unfortunately, the day never came.

He used to keep a 4½ gallon cask of vinegar in the house—to drink ! And for lighting in the house he never used anything but tallow candles.

Although he was a very rich man he hated spending his money. If cider was sold for 2d. a pint at a nearby inn, and the same article cost 1½d. at another inn a mile away, he would walk this distance. to get it.

When a demand note for rates on his property was received, or any account with coppers included, he deducted the odd pence when making the payment.

This white-bearded old gentleman who always wore a 'box' hat would not make a will because his lawyer needed payment. The lawyer told me that this very strange man was entitled to £3,000 under a will made by a relative, but as there were some legal difficulties involved the old man never got the money because he would not bear the costs to enable him to do so.

In another village I once met another farmer of quite a different calibre.

Two days after paying 'twenty golden sovereigns' for a cow he found it dead in a field, poisoned by swallowing a piece of copper wire that had fallen into a field when a lineman was cutting telephone wires.

Another cow had part of a hoof severed with a length of wire, also dropped in this field, and as he was unable to obtain milk from this cow for several weeks there was a great loss in revenue, in addition to the fees paid to the veterinary surgeon.

Yet this farmer never made a claim for damages to which he was entitled. When I asked him why he did not do so, he said: "Well, I didn't want to get the lineman into trouble."

Here was a man who was prepared to suffer his loss rather than make a claim that might bring punishment to the lineman, yet I believe, he was unjustifiably punished some weeks later when he appeared in court and was convicted of selling milk to which some evil-doer had added water!

*   *   *

In many ways I have had close connection with farming and country pursuits all my life, many of my early days being spent with grandfather who owned a farm near Ross.

As he was a very hard worker himself he believed that a little of it would be beneficial to me.

One of my earliest recollections was being given a wooden clapper in early Spring, and then having to walk up and down the furrows of a field on a raw and foggy morning using the clappers and a piping voice to scare away the rooks.

Other jobs entailing very hard work included turning the handle of machines to cut up swedes and turnips, but perhaps the hardest was the cutting of chaff.

When a workman cut standing corn with a scythe — for 2s. 6d. an acre — another of my activities was to gather it and tie it up with a few stalks of corn, but later, when a binding machine was obtained a much easier occupation was riding the front horse as the corn was cut.

One of my pleasures was in accompanying grandfather in his pony-cart to Ross market each week especially when I was allowed to hold the reins and drive the pony.

There was one public-house, just off the main road, where grandfather was in the habit of calling to have a drop of whisky, and the pony would automatically turn the corner and stop at the inn; any attempt on my part by pulling the reins to divert it was futile.

Perhaps the pony had its own reason for stopping, for it was always given a pint of stout to drink!

Although farmers do not depend entirely on good luck for their living, yet a little is a useful asset, and one I remember did benefit by this acquisition.

When he was a young man — working on his father's farm — he was forbidden by the father to drink beer, a beverage which the son enjoyed.

One day the latter was going to work in a field. Before he entered it he saw a small barrel in a ditch adjoining a road, and on inspection he found this to be a 4½ gallon barrel of beer! How it came to be there he did not know, or care, but assumed that, unknown to the driver it had fallen off a brewery wagon.

The barrel was picked up and then hidden in a hedge and, every day until the barrel was empty, the farmer's boy was able to satisfy his thirst. This was, indeed a bit of good luck, but it did not end there.

Much later in life, when he was in possession of a farm, he went to a town during the Second World War to see a merchant regarding the sale of some fruit, and to receive a cheque for what had been supplied.

99

On his land the farmer had several pear trees, the fruit from which had been allowed to rot each year as it was not considered fit for any purpose.

Before starting his journey he put a few of these pears in his pocket, more with the object of having a joke than hope of selling them. Asking the merchant if he could do with some pears he then handed him one, but as the recipient could make no impression on it with his teeth it was thrown away in disgust.

Imagine, therefore, the surprise of the farmer when he received a telephone call from the dealer a few days later offering him 11d. a pound for all the pears he had, and saying that if the farmer would pick the pears he would send a lorry for them.

The pears were picked and put in the lorry, and the farmer's intended joke resulted in the receipt of a cheque for over £100!

At the end of the war this lucky man paid £5 for a number of heavy packing cases at a war depot, and these he picked up at various times when he was in the neighbourhood with an empty lorry; the last one of these cases being much heavier than the others.

Let him describe what caused it to be so heavy: "I put it in the lorry and then made my way home. During the time I was having my dinner I wondered what made the case so heavy, so when I had finished eating decided to open it.

"What do you think was in it?" he asked me.

"Haven't the least idea," I replied.

I knew that he had enjoyed a certain measure of good luck, but when he said: "A brand new motor-cycle" I realised the true meaning of the words "wonders never cease."

*   *   *

THE FALL. A young man whose father had been hanged was faced with a Life Insurance form. After the usual questions enquiring about any hereditary diseases there was one asking for the cause of death of his parents. He wrote: "Mother died of pneumonia. Father was taking his part in a public function when the platform gave way."

THE BALANCE. A man gave instructions to a Scots undertaker to carry out the funeral arrangements in burying his mother-in-law. He was a long time paying the account, in fact there was 7/6 outstanding when the undertaker said to him: "Look here, my lad, if that balance of 7s. 6d. isn't paid by Saturday, UP she comes !"

100

When I wanted to find out something about eels some years ago I went to the men who caught elvers in the Severn, but none of them could give me any reliable information.

One man, however, did suggest that I should see an old man named Joe Carvy who lived at Framilode. "Joe," he said, "has been catching elvers, eels and salmon for over 50 years, and he knows all about 'em."

To meet a man who 'knows all' about any subject is very exceptional so I made the journey to see this very knowledgeable man at his home.

At the time of my arrival Joe was in the act of covering a wooden frame with a kind of cheesecloth to form a net, but as elvers were not expected for a few days he was pleased to spare me a little of his time to talk about them.

"But, mind you," he said "the only things I knows about 'em is what I read in a book that a gentleman gives me as a present after I 'ad learned 'im 'ow to catch salmon.

"When there was nothing to do of a winter's night I sits me down in me old armchair and reads this 'ere book, and I sort of learns it off by 'eart like."

As we were near the local inn I invited Joe to have a drop of ale and he suggested that if I put questions to him he would try to answer them.

"Well, Joe," I said, "there are some who do not believe that elvers are young eels. What do you think about this?

"There ain't any doubt about it, mister," he replied. "Them elvers be eels all right."

"Are elvers bred in the Severn?" — "No, it said in that there book that eels breed in foreign parts; somewhere around the West Indies, I think it said."

"That is a long distance from here. How do you think they get to the shores of this country?" —"Well, as I do understand it, the young 'uns when they be born be flat and something life a leaf, almost like a bit of thin glass, and as 'em do float near the surface of the water the currents washes 'em over 'ere."

"The elvers caught in the Severn which I have eaten were not flat in shape. Can you account for this?" "Yes, 'cause during the time they be coming across the water to this river they change their shape: and it might surprise you to know that they takes about three years to get 'ere!"

Joe was very anxious to tell me more about the extraordinary life of the eel, so he contined: "Do you know, mister, that after eels have lived in the country for some years and they want to breed they goes back to where they was born, and, according to that there book the female eel lays her eggs and dies."

Joe was not sure how eels were able to get into ponds, and streams

streams other than the river, but thought they must travel overland to do so.

Many people have kept elvers in water and tried to rear them to maturity, but Joe's experience in this direction had not been very successful: the longest time he had kept one alive was one year.

I told Joe that the record for the longest living eel in captivity was at one time 56 years, but this record had since been beaten by one living in an acquarium in Sweden for 88 years.

Obvioulsy the old man did not believe this when he said: "Ah! but I can tell you a true story about a eel. One day I was walking along the river bank when I spied a dead salmon lying on a sand-bank, so I picked'n up and took'n 'ome with me.

"To find out if 'e was all right to eat I takes me knife and cut'n open and darned if there wasn't a eel inside'.

"No wonder the salmon was dead, for the eel 'ad got inside'n and eaten all the intestines away!..

*   *   *

MEMORIES OF THE FOREST OF DEAN

When making a journey into the countryside I often think how fortunate are we residents of Gloucester to be living so close to beautiful surroundings.

Since my journey around the Cotswolds I have been on a trip to a vastly different type of country, travelling via Huntley and Long-hope to the Forest of Dean.

Passing through Longhope reminded me of the old saying that people 'banked their money' at this place, and also that 'pips'for placing in raspberry jam were made at the local saw-mills.

During a conversation with the late Mr. Constance, who owned the saw-mills, he told me that on one occasion he received a letter asking him to give a quotation for the 'pips'.

Many years ago the Forest of Dean contained fallow deer, limited to 800, but on my visit the most prominent animals I saw were sheep wandering on the highway, and in some places lying on the roads oblivious to traffic.

My acquaintance with the Forest miners began at the end of the last century. The conditions under which they worked were very bad, one man telling me that in the winter months the only time he saw daylight was the day he was not working—Sunday.

Most of the miners lived a considerable distance from the mines and the only method of getting to work was by walking, often through woods with no paths except those made by themselves.

Having walked a number of miles, sometimes soaked to the skin with rain, they still had a long walk to get to their 'place' after descending the pit.

In many cases the roof of their place was about 3 feet high — often less — and sometimes the men would have to kneel in water for the whole day to get at the coal.

At the end of a tiring day there would be the long walk to get home, to have a 'wash down' in front of the kitchen fire in full view of the whole family.

With little opportunity to air his wet clothes the miner would have to wear them when leaving home the next day.

As he left home early in the morning his wife, or mother, would prepare his meal the previous night and place it in his 'tommy-bag.' and also fill a bottle with tea; these the miner would put in two pockets of his coat before leaving home the next morning.

On one occasion a wife, after her husband had gone to bed, dropped the tea-bottle and broke it, but was able to find another bottle, much larger than the broken one, and fill it with tea.

When the husband came down the following morning he was unable to get this larger bottle into his pocket, and then shouted up the stairs to his wife: "Missus," I can't get this 'ere bloomin' bottle into me pocket — what shall I do?" "You darned sonky, " said the startled woman, "pour a drop of the tea out."

On the day miners received their pay butchers and fishmongers were at the top of the pit to sell their wares, and men were able to buy and take home the 'Sunday joint' or any fish they required.

In those far off days chapels were full on Sundays with miners and and their families, some of the men often acting as lay-readers or, at times, 'taking' the whole service.

One miner after conducting a morning service, was invited to have dinner with a Forest family, and when they had finished the meal he said: "Oh Lord if there be anything in I wuss (worse) than apple dumplings root it out, O Lord."

One of my most pleasant memories is of seeing 20 or 30 miners sitting on the grass in a wood on a Sunday afternoon and hearing them them singing hymns in harmony.

I have heard splendid singing by choirs in Rouen Cathedral; the Welsh National Eisteddfod and numerous other places, but nothing has ever impressed me so much as on this occasion.

Despite their very tiring labour of the week they gathered together and sang. Simple; yet so effective and sincere.

I enjoyed the splendid scenery in the Forest and the views of surrounding country from high points.

That the Forester has a sense of humour about a view can be best illustrated by a story.

A man tied his donkey to a stake at the top of a coal tip, absolutely devoid of vegetation. A friend who saw him doing this said: "Whats the good of tying the donkey there, old 'un; there's nothing there for 'un to Yut (eat)." "No replied the owner of the 'moke,' "but look at the view 'im da get."

*   *   *

THE FLYING HERO IN THE LUNATIC ASYLUM

On the Somme in France during the terrible battles of 1918— when our Battalion of the Gloucestershire Regiment was reduced by casualties from about 1,000 men to 120—I saw too much of the horror of war to want to write about it.

Despite the years that have elapsed since that time there are certain incidents, some unusual and others amusing, that I remember in connection with army life of those days.

After being put out of action and sent back to a hospital in England for three months I was sent home on sick leave for a month and told to wait for further instructions.

No instructions were received at the end of the month, or by the time the second month expired, and it seems incredible that someone at the War Office should have forgotten my existance, for it was not until I wrote at the end of the third month that the 'bras-hats' realised I was still alive!

Then came an order to proceed to another hospital in Lancashire, and on arrival at Liverpool Station a porter took all my luggage and I asked him if he could tell me how to get to Maghull hospital. He suddenly dropped the luggage, and with a look of horror on his face said: "You're not going there, sir!" I told him that was my intention and added: "Why, what's wrong with it?" "It's a lunatic asylum." he replied.

On arrival there I found that at one time it had been used for the mentally deficient but was now occupied by wounded soldiers. A patient who had been in a Chester hospital for some months was brought in on a stretcher and put in the bed next to mine. For some months he was there, most of the time in bed. He was, however, allowed to go out if he was taken in a wheel-chair, and he always wore the uniform of an R F C officer.

Varioius kind people in the village would call for him and take him to their homes for tea. So popular did he become with the ladies that he got engaged to one of them; she even persuaded him to join the church choir where her father was organist.

I, with others, took him on several occasions to Liverpool, and this meant pushing the wheel-chair to the local station—he never walked on any occasion—and using a taxi at the destination to get to the cafe for tea.

We all felt sorry for him that his journeys were made at our expense.

His stories of flying exploits were extraordinary, particulary one about getting back to base with his plane after travelling 100 miles with a bullet through his petrol tank! He ordered and received a new R F C uniform, but his cheque was returned marked R. D. The firm who supplied the uniform then started an investigation and the result of it was a revelation This man had masqueraded under a wrong name; lived in hospitals for months; had never been in the R F C or suffered from any disability. How he deceived the medical authorities will never be known.

A further revelation was that he ran away from home when a youth and went to Australia, and at the outbreak of war he returned to this country and joined the Somerset Light Infantry.

When an escort came to the hospital to take him away it was the first time I ever saw this prince of 'lead-swingers' walk.

When convalescing during the war at a house adjoining Sunningdale golf course it was my custom each morning to walk in civilian clothes to a shop and get two morning newspapers, and quite often saw the local police constable. He never spoke, but it seemed that he always looked at me with suspicion. Incidentally, it was at the time when white feathers were given to eligible men who were not in uniform.

After passing the local policeman one morning I noticed another policeman about 200 yards ahead on the road, and then saw him disappear into a gateway. It occurred to me that this was a trap so when about half way between the two I suddenly ran across the golf course, with both officers in pursuit. It was only a short distance to go, and I was inside the house when there was a loud knock on the door. The door was opened by the owner—a local magistrate—and, while I peeped from behind a curtain, he explained to the policeman who I was.

One little incident at this house caused me some amusement. The two newspapers I bought were then published by the Northcliffe Press and my host had a grudge against it for condemning a society to which he belonged.

One day I left the papers on a table, and on seeing them my host seized them with tongs and flung them into the blazing fire. He said: 'I used the tongs purposely, as I did not want to soil my fingers with such utter rubbish!!'

Some of the mistakes made by army officials and medical officers were at times confusing, and sometimes amusing.

Who could have been the 'brains' that issued an order for me six feet in height to join a Bantam Battalion at Chiseldon when I was first commissioned? Fortunately it was remedied the next day after a very embarrassing time trying to march with these small men who took a much shorter pace than mine.

Some time after the end of the war it was necessary for me to go as an in-patient to a military hospital in Bath for treatment to my ears, and on the day appointed I appeared before the chief medical officer. On his table he had a bundle of papers, and after looking through them for a few minutes he approached me and said: "What is wrong with your eyes?"

"Nothing," I said, perhaps rather abruptly. Then raising his voice he shouted: "Well what the hell have you come here for?"

When I told him, he looked at the papers again and discovered that they referred to another patient!

As he was unable to find anything regarding my case there was no alternative but to return to Gloucester.

Three weeks later a letter was received to make the journey again, and on arrival there I met a different medical officer. He had a brief look through his papers, but when he said: "Ah! you've come here about a commission in the Territorial Army." I didn't know whether to laugh or cry. After a search lasting about two hours the correct papers were found and all was well, at last. The following day, being Sunday. I played the organ for the morning service, without any discordant note I hope.

*   *   *

A WARNING TO DOG BREEDERS

If a dealer wants to sell a dog that has won prizes at dog shows he (or she) puts great emphasis on this, but before purchasing any dog so advertised it is a good thing for a prospective buyer to ascertain the type of show where the dog was exhibited, and the nature of the competition it had to contend with. Sometimes at the very small shows there are only one or two dogs in the classes, and if a dog wins in these it may not be a particularly good specimen. Some exhibitors will travel long distances to obtain these prize cards, even if the cash value is very small.

One of the many instances I recall was at a small members' show where I was an exhibitor. Sitting next to me at the ringside was a very well-known judge and exhibitor who had travelled nearly 100 miles in the car of the judge for this show. During a conversation with him I asked him if he had brought a dog with him, and he informed me that he had not; it was certainly not in the hall at the time. After all the classes but one had been judged I was astounded to see this man and his dog appear in the "Any Variety, Open Class," where the dog was awarded the first prize, and also the award for best in show. Later on I discovered that after the dog had been passed by the veterinary surgeon before judging commenced it had been placed in its box in the car outside. This I thought was very sharp practice, and difficult to understand when the value of the prize was a mere fifteen shillings !

A dealer in Pembroke bought one of my bitches in whelp, with the stipulation that he would give me one of the bitch puppies if the dam produced a litter containing any.

As he did not write and inform me if the bitch had whelped I wrote to him about six weeks after the due date. His reply was that the bitch had seven puppies, three dogs and four bitches, but all the bitches had died ! No thought of asking me to accept a dog puppy! The tone of my reply to him probably inferred that I did not accept his explanation, and he then invited me to visit his kennels about 100 miles away. What hope should I have had of ascertaining the truth from a man whose notepaper had the headlines: "Over a hundred dogs in stock?"

During the last war there was much profiteering in many things but never more so than one instance I knew concerning the sale of dogs. Quite close to some kennels was a camp for American soldiers and when some of these men saw four cocker spaniels in the garden adjoining they purchased them, paving over £20 for each. These puppies had no pedigree, and one I saw was a dreadful specimen of the breed. The dealer did not breed them, he bought them and when he told me that he had paid eleven shillings each for them I estimated that this was about their true value !

Not far from this camp a man owned a non-pedigree type of terrier, and because it had bitten a postman on two occasions he decided to get rid of it. A few miles away lived an unscrupulous dealer who would purchase any kind of dog, and he bought this particular terrier for a very small amount of money. Incredible though it may seem, this dealer not only sold the dog to another person living in the same district from whence it came but he also handed the purchaser a faked pedigree !

At one show I encountered a glaring instance of the faked pedigree, for which the exhibitor of the dog was entirely blameless. When she purchased it from a breeder he gave her a pedigree with it, and she registered it at the Kennel Club before showing it. I noticed in the catalogue that this dog—according to the pedigree—had been sired by my own stud dog, but on seeing the breeder's name I knew that this man had never made use of my dog. Upon investigation it was ascertained that by some means this breeder had secured one of my stud cards—which contained the dog's pedigree—and made use of this when making out a pedigree for the dog he sold!

*   *   *

BULLS EYE. "Oh, look, Mummy! There's a cow tossing Daddy in the air." "Don't be silly dear. That's not a cow - it's a bull."

107

DOG BREEDING HAZARDS

When first attempting to breed dogs I did so with the thought, that it might afford me a very pleasant pastime, and it was in this frame of mind that I secured a brood bitch, pure-bred but of un-certain pedigree. After waiting four months until she was ready for mating I then sent her away to a well-known dog, and paid a sub-stantial stud fee for the service. I soon discovered that it needs a lot of patience and time seemed to pass very slowly as I waited for the 'happy event.'

My excitement knew no bounds when the first puppy made an appearance, and then another, but the bitch was so long in labour that when two others arrived a day later the mother must have been in such pain that she killed all of them! This was a very dis-appointing start to my venture so I gave the bitch away and bought another, thinking it was no use giving up after falling at the first obstacle. Such a thing couldn't happen again, so I thought.

There was another long wait before the new arrival could be mated, and when this was done another long period had to elapse before the litter arrived. The birth of these puppies I shall not for-get. There were six of them, and as each one appeared the mother swallowed it!!

This was very discouraging for a beginner, and it seemed that luck was running against me, but remembering the old saying of 'third time lucky' I found a good home for this cannibal and bought yet another bitch at a cost of £45. But the third time did not prove lucky, for after having this bitch mated on two occasions she was found to be a non-breeder! It was no use keeping this animal so, after spending more money on displayed advertisements in the doggy papers she was sold for a mere £8. Apart form the loss of money in buying these bitches, paying stud fees, feeding, etc., nearly two years had elapsed without having obtained any stock, but despite these misfortunes it didn't act as a deterrent for I happened to be one who thinks 'there is always something around the corner.'

I therefore bought another bitch and had her mated when the time arrived and then, like Mr. Micawber 'waited for something to turn up.' Surely, after a long and trying apprenticeship patiently borne the tide of fortune must turn in my favour this time! But despite my optimism the result of this mating proved negative.

After so many misfortunes it needed more than the patience attributed to Job to continue my efforts to secure some results, but now I decided to retain this bitch and make one one last attempt to succeed. Months of waiting again for the mating and the coming of the litter (if any), and then at last there was success, if only a minor one. Two puppies arrived ! One was a perfect specimen, but the other was so malformed that it had to be destroyed. So for the outlay in money in the attempt to breed dogs amounted to over £100, and the result of this—just one live puppy!

Seven months after it was born I exhibited it at a dog show, and greatly to my surprise it won two first prizes competing against sixteen others in the 'Any Variety Classes.' Here was some reward to compensate for all the disasters of the past, but ill-luck came again when it died of distemper a month later!

Undeterred by the foregoing adverse circumstances I continued to buy other bitches, and in the years following the tide did turn and I was able to breed some litters of puppies, many of which gained successes when exhibited at shows.

On one occasion I exhibited a puppy where the judge took a liking to it and wanted to buy it, but when a woman exhibitor knew of this she also offered a price for it, but in each case the offer was refused.

Imagine my surprise when the woman exhibitor arrived at my house two days later. She had driven 150 miles—and said she had come to buy the dog. I still had no thought of selling it, but after much wheedling by this enterprising woman I very reluctantly named a price, and she paid it. It was obvious that she was very delighted when she put the dog in her car, but no words can describe my thoughts as she bade me farewell with these parting words: "I think you've given this dog away!"

These incidents may act as a warning to anyone purchasing a dog. If a puppy is needed the best method of obtaining one is to consult a breeder with a good reputation, and if he, or she, has some for sale it may be possible to see the sire and dam of the litter; this will give some indication of what the puppy will look like when it reaches maturity. Women particularly, when they see very small puppies in some pet shops fall in love with them, using such terms as "adorable" and "beautiful", but caution should be used here for many of these creatures grow up to be monstrosities!!!

*   *   *

HORSEY DIOCESE. "And what was the collection for to-day, Mary ?" asked the lady of her maid as she came back from church. "Summat about aidin' the dyin' osses fund, mum, s'far as I could gather."

GOOD OLD DAYS. For varied requirements at a cheap rate, it would be hard to beat the following old-time advertisement. "Wanted for drapers house in the City, as a porter, an athletic man of serious countenance, a good character and the Lady Huntingdon persuasion; must attend prayers twice a day and Divine Service four times on Sundays, be able to bear confinement, havethe fear of God before his eyes and be able to carry two hundred-weight. Wages fourteen shillings a week and find himself."

JAKE – A POACHER

Did you ever hear of a Solicitor accompanying a poacher on a nightly expedition ? Jake, the poacher, had appeared before the Magistrates on several occasions for various offences, and was well-always represented by a well-known local lawyer. It was just after the termination of one of the cases that he expressed a desire to accompany Jake on one of his nocturnal visits, and arrangements were made for them to go on Christmas Eve to one of his favourite hunting grounds. It may have been the spirit of adventure when the lawyer expressed his desire, for it was a great risk for a man who was so versed in the law and its consequences, and was so prominent in the Town.

The night chosen for the adventure was a particularly wet one, and this did not augur well for the night's outing. Jake told me afterwards that he was sorry he ever agreed to the arrangement, for on their arrival at the rabbit warrens the incessant talking of the lawyer, and his anxiety to return home again, ruined the chance of catching anything, so it was decided to pack up and go home.

Not wishing to return over the same route Jake then chose to get to the main road by putting a plank (that had been hidden by Jake) over a narrow stream. The plank was placed in position, but no amount of persuasion would induce his legal companion to walk across it. The only thing for Jake to do was to carry his unwilling passenger on his back, and it does not want much imagination to picture the 15 stone Jake struggling across with his burden on a very slippery plank ! In describing this to me Jake said: "I've 'eard it said that it is a good thing to 'ave the law on your side but it's a damned nuisance on your back!"

Jake contended that all animals were wild, and as it was a free country his method of obtaining them were perfectly legitimat, and it was only a craving in his stomach for food that made him want to satisfy his hunger. He was a very strong and agile man, with a quickness of eye and freedom of foot that was remarkable, and this, added to an alertness of mind gave him a great advantage over his biggest enemies the police.

Cunning though he was Jake met his equal on one occasion. He set out one night on his bicycle to one of his favourite haunts, where he caught a dozen rabbits; these he placed under some straw near a rick of hay to be picked up later, and then cycled home again. Early the following morning he drove in his pony-cart to collect the rabbits - but they had disappeared !

Although he searched carefully over the ground he could not find them, and it wasn't until daybreak that he thought the mystery had been solved. In an adjoining field was the caravan of some gipsies - employed by a farmer to pull up swedes - and hanging singly on the outside of the caravan were ten rabbits, and Jake had no doubt where they had been obtained, but he couldn't claim them. He did, however, have a chat with the gipsies, cooking two rabbits at the time, but when they asked him if he would like a meal he hastened away before he could give vent to his thoughts.

One of the favourite places used by the police for intercepting poachers was a bridge which crossed a river. Early one morning Jake was pulled up in his pony-cart by a policeman, and then told that he was in possession of game; this was denied, and the 'copper' was was asked to search the cart. This he did, but found nothing inside. When the constable saw a large bulging pocket of Jake he said: "What have you got in your pockets ?" "MUSHROOMS", replied Jake, and then the old man produced large handfuls of leaves, much to the annoyance of the law. Had the constable made a more accurate search of the pony-cart he would have found a pheasant and some rabbits in a false bottom of the cart!

Our garden was cultivated by Jake and I used to go into the shed with him when he was having a meal; he told me about many events and about birds and animals of the countryside. I once suggested to him that poachers were considered as bad men, and that indeed raised his ire. He said: "Just because I've killed a few rabbits I be considered bad, but them chaps what do make atom bombs to kill thousands of 'uman beings is supposed to be doing good !! It don't make no sense to me !!

One of his early adventures had been to run away from school, go home and get one of his mother's dinner forks and tie it to a long stick. He had seen a salmon lying in shallow water and, just as he was going to spear it, who should come on the scene but the water bailiff ! Jake was reported to the schoolmaster and, knowing that when he went to school the next morning he would be getting several cuts on the behind with a cane, he was artful enough to put on two pairs of trousers. Of course he had a bigger hiding for this, but he laughed as he told me how he got his own back. "I chucked a blooming inkwell at the teacher" he said, "and its a good job 'e didn't try to duck 'is 'ead, or the inkwell might have gone through the window."

When I asked Jake what he thought about modern poachers he said: "Some's good; some's bad; some's better than t'others, and some's no good at all." Poaching is one of the noblest professions there is !

A covey of partridges in a field was doomed if seen by the ever watchful Jake. Leaning on the gate of a field—where he could be seen by the birds—he would give an occasional tap-tap with his pipe on the top of the gate. As long as he remained there doing this birds would not move. At dusk the figure of the old poacher would make very slowly over the grass, and on these unsuspecting birds he would drop a net that had been made for that purpose.

This man had a very kind heart, for he often gave rabbits to poor people in the village who were in need of food.

When he was a young man he had an unusual accident when ferreting for rabbits. He put his gun on the ground when he pulled a rabbit out of a hole, and as there was another one in the hole he wrung the neck of the first rabbit and tossed it to land unfortunately on the gun. With its dying kick the rabbit's leg came in contact with the trigger of the gun, and Jake received a quantity of shot in his buttocks, for which he had to go to the hospital for weeks. Never again in his life did he use a gun, relying, he said: "on me 'ead and me 'ands, and a jolly good dog." And Jake always had a very exceptional dog.

Years ago I was near a public-house. Jake had been fishing on the other side of the river, and had landed from a flat-bottomed boat to get some refreshment at the Inn. Suddenly he remembered that he had left his pipe on the stump of a tree where he had been sitting, and he said to the dog: "Thee go and fetch my pipe and mind thee dusn't get'n wet," and sure enough the dog did what it was asked to do. When we were having a drink Jake told me that he had been robbed by a London firm for some moles he had sent them. During the winter he had set traps and caught 75 moles, then had to skin them and 'dress' before putting them on an old door to dry. And what did he receive from this firm ? One farthing each !!

His method of catching ducks was a good one, as he relates: "You want to be a good swimmer to catch ducks, and the best time to do it is when the moon is up. Just before it becomes dark I take cover under a bush down close to the edge of a pond, and stay there and watch the ducks drop on to the water. When they've finished I take off me clothes and rub badger fat all over me body to keep out the cold. I ties a bag around my waist, and then puts a piece of metal tubing, about 18 inches long, between me teeth, bent into shape so that one part be above me 'ead and I can then breathe when I be under water. I gets into the pond very quietly and swim under them ducks, then collars, 'em by the legs and puts 'em in the bag,"

"One rough winter's night, "Jake said, "I fixed a long net over there near the copse, and then took me dog to the t'other side of the field to drive some rabbits towards the net. When I got near to the net I 'eard a noise going on just as if 'ell 'ad been let loose ! Instead of they rabbits been in there be dam'nd if it was'nt a blooming badger — and the dog — and there they was locked together and all wrapped up in the net, and I 'ad to get me knife out cut the net to pieces afore I could save the dog from being chewed up !!"

"Early one morning " he continued, I was on the land carrying 'alf a dozen rabbits which I 'ad catched, and was making me way towards a gate when I spied a 'copper' standing on the road t'other side of the gate. I know'd 'e was'nt there to wish me good morning so I stopped my side of the gate to see what would 'appen. The farmer 'ad give me permission to catch the rabbits, so I was safe enough, but just for a bit of a lark I took to me 'eels and ran across the field, and darned me if he didn't come tearin' after me; then I popped through a gap in the fence and got on the road. There 'appened to be a bull in the field, and when the copper saw'n 'e went like 'ell for leather towards a fence, and the last I saw of 'im 'e was 'anging from some barbed wire that 'ad caught

112

in the seat of 'is pants!! That's what 'appens to people what don't mind their own business."

Whatever his faults Jake had his own particular brand of humour and an incident when he was living near the river bears evidence of this. He incurred a debt, and because of his non-payment a bailiff was put in possession of his cottage. He informed the man that if he would wait for half an hour he could get the necessary cash from a friend in the village. Jake left the house with no thought about the money ! A better idea had occurred to him. He kept bees, and that morning he had taken a swarm and put them in a skep. Unseen by the bailiff he placed a ladder against the wall of the cottage and then ascended and placed the skep of bees upside down on the only chimney. Hurriedly descending he then took away the ladder and sought refuge in a shed to watch the result of his handiwork. Within ten minutes the frightened bailiff — no doubt stung into action — shot out of the cottage doorway surrounded by the angry bees, and Jake swore to me that the man dived into the river to rid himself of them ! !

On Christmas Eve Jake went into a public-house, and when he came out he saw a big black and white rabbit in a hutch in the yard. Thinking he would like something for his Xmas dinner he pulled out the rabbit and placed it in his pocket. Unknown to Jake, the landlord told the village constable and suggested the possible culprit. On Xmas day, just before Jake had finished his cooking, he heard a voice wishing him the compliments of the season. On looking up he was surprised to see the village policeman looking in through the open window.

"Something good you be cooking, " said the limb of the law. "Smells like rabbit." "Sure it is," said Jake, "come in and have a mouthful." The invitation was accepted, and during the meal, the constable noted the large size of the rabbit and expressed his opinion that it was a fine specimen. "I'll bet he had a lovely skin," he said, and then asked whether he could have it. When Jake asked what was the use of an old rabbit skin, he was told it could be cured and dressed, and then made into a pair of gloves for one of his children. "What a pity you didn't come in afore," said Jake. "If only I'd known you'd want it I'd certainly have kept it for you." The constable, now very doubtful about the help he was getting with the investigation, said "Why, what have you done with it?" "Well," siad Jake, "it's like this here. Whenever I have rabbit for my dinner I always eat the skin first.'

When I last saw him in his cottage there was a long net for catching rabbits hanging from a nail in the wall, the only thing he possessed in connection with his 'art', and when I asked him why he kept it now that he was no longer able to use it, he replied. "When it's time for me to go sir, I 'ope somebody will put it in me coffin, 'cause there might be some rabbits to catch in the other country I be goin' to'"

*   *   *

STORIES

The new Vicar's wife was a highly educated literary woman, and was inclined to put it over the parishioners. At a social, when speaking to Mrs. Brown, whose husband kept the Falcon Inn, she enquired: "Do you like Shakespeare ?" Mrs Brown was not to be done. "I've no time to read politics, but I've got a **piece** of red flannel where I wants it."

A man who committed a serious crime was put on a 'hot-plate' and electrocuted, and to commemorate the occasion his widow puts a wreath every year on a fuse box.

Going into a bank and giving the cashier a piece of paper a man said: "Cash this quickly as I am in a hurry." It was a cheque for a penny! The cashier said : "How would you like it head or tail !"

When a little girl was introduced to her triplet sisters for the first time, she turned to her mother and said: "It's your own fault, mummy you shouldn't have sent daddy to order a baby — you know how he stutters."

Old lady to busdriver, who was signalling with his arms in the usual way to show which turning he was about to take: "Look here, young man you keep your 'ands on that there steering wheel — I'll tell you when its raining."

A schoolteacher asked a boy what he knew about Solomon's wives, and the bright boy replied: "King Solomon had three hundred wives, and seven hundred cucumbers. He was a wise man and slept with his father.

A man due to illness, was unable to go to work in the office of a firm, and his wife sent the following telegram: "Regret my husband cannot come to the office today. He is in bed with two trained nurses."

When Mary brought in a glass to her mistress, she carried the glass in her hand. "When you bring in the milk tomorrow, Mary, will you please bring it in on a tray." Next evening, Mary arrived, complete with tray, but no glass. "I've brought a spoon, mum, 'cos I wasn't sure if you lapped it up."

During a debate on foreign affairs in the House of Commons. A member, puzzled as to the exact position of the Virgin Islands, asked the Prime Minister for information. "I really do not know" he replied "but I imagine they must be a long way from the Isle of Man;"

*   *   *

A LETTER RECEIVED AFTER A BROADCAST FROM LONDON

My first attempt at this method of putting over a story was when meeting a producer from the Bristol Studio on the bowling green at Painswick. He listened to my weak attempt to 'tell him the tale about certain events in the Forest of Dean, and then promised to write to me, which he did, asking me to send him a script containing some Forest stories.

This story, called "No fools in that Forest" was done to the best of my ability, and from there I again appeared with another broadcast containing Charles Cole as the Chairman, H.S. Joyce from Barnstable, and Arthur Ponchaud, in the programme entitled "Round about the animal world." Arthur (who was a taxidermist) talked about some funny things at his home. A kitten with eight legs and two bodies - a tiny pig with eight legs, and a calf with two heads. One of the most interesting freaks was a lamb with three eyes—two normal and one in the centre of the forehead. He had just skinned a large pike which had swallowed a water vole, a good sized roach, and a box of Swan Vesta matches ! Also, a barn owl's stomach that had 10 shrews and a common wren in it.

The next broardcast I did was "Where I Live" (Gloucester), in a programme for the children of Gloucester.

Then when I went to live in London for a short time, I appeared at the B.B.C. London and did "Were those the good old days, " "The game of bowls," in the Indian Summer programme, and "Village Cricket," "Odd Jobs", and "Bird Watching" in the "Home This Afternoon" programme.

After broadcasting "The Game of Bowls" a most unusual letter was received from Portsmouth, undated, unsigned, and no address.

Dear Mr. Stanley Bennett,

I listened to your little talk on the B.B.C. this afternoon, and I thought I would like to make a few observations.

I am an O.A.P. and my age is 76 turned, and I may as well tell you how nimble I am.

(1) I suffer from Myopia which is a very gradual blindness and also have Arthritus in a toe of the left foot. The Myopia means I cannot read newspaper print tho I may see some of these awful advertisements, the very large ones of which I am utterly uninterested . . . I use a portable typewriter, and learnt the sequence of the letters quite a long time ago, when the snow was on this year I fell and Dr. said I had a minor paralysis, I am fairly good now but inclined to drag my feet, and like at times to use a stick, this is useful for finding the curb and keeping upright on the disgraceful pavements, no attention is paid to level the path, but of course thats nothing we are only old folk and time we were gone is apparently the attitude of the local authorities. I add that bad pavements have been the cause of very

many falls, the painting of the curb in a contrasting colour to a crossing or an entrance doesn't enter the brains or the heads of these men who are responsible.

Now for the arthritus, its just hell, I can go out for awhile but it comes on if I am on my feet, this means that I go into a shop and more or less rush out too quickly before I find out if they have cheated me. So you can imagine me having a GO at Bowls.

Now I can just see you a bouncing 65 or might be less, its all very well for you to show off, what you can do, if you are a well to do bachelor its grand, somebody is doing chores for you, but perhaps you are married and in that case if both of you 65ers you might by a fluke both be nimble on your feet, but how many couples retain their health so that both of you can have a go and show off there are not many to speak of.

There is the shopping, the preparing of food, the cooking and the washing up and drying up, then there is the house work and the mending of your socks and your wifes clothes or are you exceptionally lucky in having a slave to get down on her knees to wash and perhaps polish the floors. If you do not know how to do these things ask your wife to teach you, and you might be as clever at throwing the wood. Do not sit on your behind reading the newspapers, your wife might pass out and then what are you going to do. I make a guess sit and moan and get some neighbour to come.

Besides all this you want a suit and vests and lots of other things, and you expect your wife to dodge about and buy them, and almost get run over chasing across the road. Of course if you have a car you must be smart and dodge the traffic, and for safetys sake let your wife sit in the back seat like the P.M. does, you or rather your wife will stand a better chance, and again TIME marches on, and its a devilish nuisanse when your sight and feet begin to irritate you, doctors can't do anything for arthritus and even your sight, that will get tiresome too, those swindlers who play with your feet they can't help either. I speak from experience. Experience is a great education. If you find your hearing is going as well, that is another nuisance. I had a second cousin who lived to 105½ years, so you see I am only a youngster, her voice faded but mine is good and strong tho I find that folk think I am Oh! so old that is because I carry a stick for just this confounded toe.

I daresay I could have it cut off, that's not unknown by any means. You may say what about the Welfare ?????? Yes that's just what I say. What about them... to be candid NOTHING, Nuffield too, why Nothing also. Home help, Nothing too, in fact a GRAND SLAM. Should be done away with altogether.

Don't forget to learn your lessons, you might make a jolly good chef an antidote to throwing that Wood. Come to the micaphone when you are 76 who does the gardening? Fumbling about with seedlings on ones knees. From Time Immemorial it has been a case of Brute Force the woman has been the worker . . she can carry a baby on her back and be pregnant too and tend the fields, whilst the males are playing cards, shove halfpenny and feathers in their heads dancing around, whilst the women work, resulting that women have more brains. Today the men bang each others heads about, go in for anything they think clever to fill their time, you can think out surely all the other stupid things they do, Men are jealous very jealous of the knowledge, unknown to them, that are natural to women, so we have scientific twaddle designed to end this universe . . its so clever . . especially with guns great guns to execute mass murder . . perhaps it's just as well . . this planet can't go on for ever, and thank goodness we including you can't live for ever!!

*　　　*　　　*

Sir Winston Churchill wrote :—

"Let us be contented with what has happened to us and be thankful for all we have been spared. Let us treasure our joys, but not bewail our sorrows."

"GOOD BYE"

Wilfred Shadbolt at Cheltenham Opera House